EDUCATION AND THE
SIGNIFICANCE OF LIFE

J. KRISHNAMURTI

EDUCATION AND THE
SIGNIFICANCE OF LIFE

HarperOne
An Imprint of HarperCollins*Publishers*

HarperOne

HarperCollins books may be purchased for educational, business, or sales promotional use. For information please write: Special Markets Department, HarperCollins Publishers, 10 East 53rd Street, New York, NY 10022.

HarperCollins Web site: http://www.harpercollins.com

HarperCollins®, 📖®, and HarperOne™ are trademarks of HarperCollins Publishers.

First Harper & Row paperback edition published in 1981.

Library of Congress Cataloging-in-Publication Data
Krishnamurti, Jiddu, 1895–
    Education and significance of life.
    1. Krishnamurti, Jiddu, 1985–. 2. Education—Addresses, essays, lectures. I. Title.
LB875.K74E38   1981   370   53–10971
ISBN 978–0–06–064876–3

11 12 RRD(H) 38 37 36 35 34 33 32 31

CONTENTS

EDUCATION AND THE
SIGNIFICANCE OF LIFE

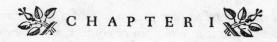

CHAPTER I

EDUCATION AND THE
SIGNIFICANCE OF LIFE

WHEN one travels around the world, one notices to what an extraordinary degree human nature is the same, whether in India or America, in Europe or Australia. This is especially true in colleges and universities. We are turning out, as if through a mould, a type of human being whose chief interest is to find security, to become somebody important, or to have a good time with as little thought as possible.

Conventional education makes independent thinking extremely difficult. Conformity leads to mediocrity. To be different from the group or to resist environment is not easy and is often risky as long as we worship success. The urge to be successful, which is the pursuit of reward whether in the material or in the so-called spiritual sphere, the search for inward or outward security, the desire for comfort—this whole process smothers discontent, puts an end to spontaneity and breeds fear; and fear blocks the intelligent understanding of life. With increasing age, dullness of mind and heart sets in.

In seeking comfort, we generally find a quiet corner in life where there is a minimum of conflict, and then we are afraid to step out of that seclusion. This fear of life, this fear of struggle and of new experience, kills in us the spirit of adventure; our whole upbringing and education have made us afraid to be different from our neighbour, afraid to think contrary to the established pattern of society, falsely respectful of authority and tradition.

Fortunately, there are a few who are in earnest, who are willing to examine our human problems without the prejudice of the right or of the left; but in the vast majority of us, there is no real spirit of discontent, of revolt. When we yield uncomprehendingly to environment, any spirit of revolt that we may have had dies down, and our responsibilities soon put an end to it.

Revolt is of two kinds: there is violent revolt, which is mere reaction, without understanding, against the existing order; and there is the deep psychological revolt of intelligence. There are many who revolt against the established orthodoxies only to fall into new orthodoxies, further illusions and concealed self-indulgences. What generally happens is that we break away from one group or set of ideals and join another group, take up other ideals, thus creating a new pattern of thought against which we will again have to revolt. Reaction only breeds opposition, and reform needs further reform.

But there is an intelligent revolt which is not reaction,

and which comes with self-knowledge through the awareness of one's own thought and feeling. It is only when we
face experience as it comes and do not avoid disturbance
that we keep intelligence highly awakened; and intelligence
highly awakened is intuition, which is the only true guide
in life.

Now, what is the significance of life? What are we living
and struggling for? If we are being educated merely to
achieve distinction, to get a better job, to be more efficient,
to have wider domination over others, then our lives will be
shallow and empty. If we are being educated only to be
scientists, to be scholars wedded to books, or specialists
addicted to knowledge, then we shall be contributing to the
destruction and misery of the world.

Though there *is* a higher and wider significance to life,
of what value is our education if we never discover it? We
may be highly educated, but if we are without deep integration of thought and feeling, our lives are incomplete,
contradictory and torn with many fears; and as long as
education does not cultivate an integrated outlook on life,
it has very little significance.

In our present civilization we have divided life into so
many departments that education has very little meaning,
except in learning a particular technique or profession. Instead of awakening the integrated intelligence of the individual, education is encouraging him to conform to a
pattern and so is hindering his comprehension of himself as
a total process. To attempt to solve the many problems of
existence at their respective levels, separated as they are into

various categories, indicates an utter lack of comprehension.

The individual is made up of different entities, but to emphasize the differences and to encourage the development of a definite type leads to many complexities and contradictions. Education should bring about the integration of these separate entities—for without integration, life becomes a series of conflicts and sorrows. Of what value is it to be trained as lawyers if we perpetuate litigation? Of what value is knowledge if we continue in our confusion? What significance has technical and industrial capacity if we use it to destroy one another? What is the point of our existence if it leads to violence and utter misery? Though we may have money or are capable of earning it, though we have our pleasures and our organized religions, we are in endless conflict.

We must distinguish between the personal and the individual. The personal is the accidental; and by the accidental I mean the circumstances of birth, the environment in which we happen to have been brought up, with its nationalism, superstitions, class distinctions and prejudices. The personal or accidental is but momentary, though that moment may last a lifetime; and as the present system of education is based on the personal, the accidental, the momentary, it leads to perversion of thought and the inculcation of self-defensive fears.

All of us have been trained by education and environment to seek personal gain and security, and to fight for ourselves. Though we cover it over with pleasant phrases, we have been educated for various professions within a system which is based on exploitation and acquisitive fear. Such a training must inevitably bring confusion and misery to ourselves and to the world, for it creates in each individual those psychological barriers which separate and hold him apart from others.

Education is not merely a matter of training the mind. Training makes for efficiency, but it does not bring about completeness. A mind that has merely been trained is the continuation of the past, and such a mind can never discover the new. That is why, to find out what is right education, we will have to inquire into the whole significance of living.

To most of us, the meaning of life as a whole is not of primary importance, and our education emphasizes secondary values, merely making us proficient in some branch of knowledge. Though knowledge and efficiency are necessary, to lay chief emphasis on them only leads to conflict and confusion.

There is an efficiency inspired by love which goes far beyond and is much greater than the efficiency of ambition; and without love, which brings an integrated understanding of life, efficiency breeds ruthlessness. Is this not what is actually taking place all over the world? Our present education is geared to industrialization and war, its principal aim being to develop efficiency; and we are caught in this machine of ruthless competition and mutual destruction. If education leads to war, if it teaches us to destroy or be destroyed, has it not utterly failed?

To bring about right education, we must obviously understand the meaning of life as a whole, and for that we have to be able to think, not consistently, but directly and truly. A consistent thinker is a thoughtless person, because he conforms to a pattern; he repeats phrases and thinks in a groove. We cannot understand existence abstractly or theoretically. To understand life is to understand ourselves, and that is both the beginning and the end of education.

Education is not merely acquiring knowledge, gathering and correlating facts; it is to see the significance of life as a whole. But the whole cannot be approached through the part—which is what governments, organized religions and authoritarian parties are attempting to do.

The function of education is to create human beings who are integrated and therefore intelligent. We may take degrees and be mechanically efficient without being intelligent. Intelligence is not mere information; it is not derived from books, nor does it consist of clever self-defensive responses and aggressive assertions. One who has not studied may be more intelligent than the learned. We have made examinations and degrees the criterion of intelligence and have developed cunning minds that avoid vital human issues. Intelligence is the capacity to perceive the essential, the *what is*; and to awaken this capacity, in oneself and in others, is education.

Education should help us to discover lasting values so that we do not merely cling to formulas or repeat slogans; it should help us to break down our national and social barriers, instead of emphasizing them, for they breed antagonism between man and man. Unfortunately, the present system of education is making us subservient, mechanical and deeply thoughtless; though it awakens us intellectually, inwardly it leaves us incomplete, stultified and uncreative.

Without an integrated understanding of life, our individual and collective problems will only deepen and extend. The purpose of education is not to produce mere scholars, technicians and job hunters, but integrated men and women who are free of fear; for only between such human beings can there be enduring peace.

It is in the understanding of ourselves that fear comes to an end. If the individual is to grapple with life from moment to moment, if he is to face its intricacies, its miseries and sudden demands, he must be infinitely pliable and therefore free of theories and particular patterns of thought.

Education should not encourage the individual to conform to society or to be negatively harmonious with it, but help him to discover the true values which come with unbiased investigation and self-awareness. When there is no self-knowledge, self-expression becomes self-assertion, with all its aggressive and ambitious conflicts. Education should awaken the capacity to be self-aware and not merely indulge in gratifying self-expression.

What is the good of learning if in the process of living we are destroying ourselves? As we are having a series of devastating wars, one right after another, there is obviously something radically wrong with the way we bring up our children. I think most of us are aware of this, but we do not know how to deal with it.

Systems, whether educational or political, are not changed

mysteriously; they are transformed when there is a fundamental change in ourselves. The individual is of first
importance, not the system; and as long as the individual
does not understand the total process of himself, no system,
whether of the left or of the right, can bring order and peace
to the world.

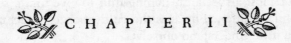

CHAPTER II

THE RIGHT KIND OF EDUCATION

THE ignorant man is not the unlearned, but he who does not know himself, and the learned man is stupid when he relies on books, on knowledge and on authority to give him understanding. Understanding comes only through self-knowledge, which is awareness of one's total psychological process. Thus education, in the true sense, is the understanding of oneself, for it is within each one of us that the whole of existence is gathered.

What we now call education is a matter of accumulating information and knowledge from books, which anyone can do who can read. Such education offers a subtle form of escape from ourselves and, like all escapes, it inevitably creates increasing misery. Conflict and confusion result from our own wrong relationship with people, things and ideas, and until we understand that relationship and alter it, mere learning, the gathering of facts and the acquiring of various skills, can only lead us to engulfing chaos and destruction.

As society is now organized, we send our children to

school to learn some technique by which they can eventually earn a livelihood. We want to make the child first and foremost a specialist, hoping thus to give him a secure economic position. But does the cultivation of a technique enable us to understand ourselves?

While it is obviously necessary to know how to read and write, and to learn engineering or some other profession, will technique give us the capacity to understand life? Surely, technique is secondary; and if technique is the only thing we are striving for, we are obviously denying what is by far the greater part of life.

Life is pain, joy, beauty, ugliness, love, and when we understand it as a whole, at every level, that understanding creates its own technique. But the contrary is not true: technique can never bring about creative understanding.

Present-day education is a complete failure because it has over-emphasized technique. In over-emphasizing technique we destroy man. To cultivate capacity and efficiency without understanding life, without having a comprehensive perception of the ways of thought and desire, will only make us increasingly ruthless, which is to engender wars and jeopardize our physical security. The exclusive cultivation of technique has produced scientists, mathematicians, bridge builders, space conquerors; but do they understand the total process of life? Can any specialist experience life as a whole? Only when he ceases to be a specialist.

Technological progress does solve certain kinds of problems for some people at one level, but it introduces wider and deeper issues too. To live at one level, disregarding the total process of life, is to invite misery and destruction. The greatest need and most pressing problem for every individual is to have an integrated comprehension of life, which will enable him to meet its ever-increasing complexities.

Technical knowledge, however necessary, will in no way resolve our inner, psychological pressures and conflicts; and it is because we have acquired technical knowledge without understanding the total process of life that technology has become a means of destroying ourselves. The man who knows how to split the atom but has no love in his heart becomes a monster.

We choose a vocation according to our capacities; but will the following of a vocation lead us out of conflict and confusion? Some form of technical training seems necessary; but when we have become engineers, physicians, accountants—then what? Is the practice of a profession the fulfilment of life? Apparently with most of us it is. Our various professions may keep us busy for the greater part of our existence; but the very things that we produce and are so entranced with are causing destruction and misery. Our attitudes and values make of things and occupations the instruments of envy, bitterness and hate.

Without understanding ourselves, mere occupation leads to frustration, with its inevitable escapes through all kinds of mischievous activities. Technique without understanding leads to enmity and ruthlessness, which we cover up with pleasant-sounding phrases. Of what value is it to emphasize technique and become efficient entities if the result is mutual destruction? Our technical progress is fantastic, but it has only increased our powers of destroying one another, and there is starvation and misery in every land. We are not peaceful and happy people.

When function is all-important, life becomes dull and boring, a mechanical and sterile routine from which we escape into every kind of distraction. The accumulation of facts and the development of capacity, which we call education, has deprived us of the fulness of integrated life and action. It is because we do not understand the total process of life that we cling to capacity and efficiency, which thus assume overwhelming importance. But the whole cannot be understood through the part; it can be understood only through action and experience.

Another factor in the cultivation of technique is that it gives us a sense of security, not only economic, but psychological as well. It is reassuring to know that we are capable and efficient. To know that we can play the piano or build a house gives us a feeling of vitality, of aggressive independence; but to emphasize capacity because of a desire for psychological security is to deny the fulness of life. The whole content of life can never be foreseen, it must be experienced anew from moment to moment; but we are afraid of the unknown, and so we establish for ourselves psychological zones of safety in the form of systems, techniques and beliefs. As long as we are seeking inward security, the total process of life cannot be understood.

The right kind of education, while encouraging the learning of a technique, should accomplish something which is of far greater importance: it should help man to experience the integrated process of life. It is this experiencing that will put capacity and technique in their right place. If one really has something to say, the very saying of it creates its own style; but learning a style without inward experiencing can only lead to superficiality.

Throughout the world, engineers are frantically designing machines which do not need men to operate them. In a life run almost entirely by machines, what is to become of human beings? We shall have more and more leisure without knowing wisely how to employ it, and we shall seek escape through knowledge, through enfeebling amusements, or through ideals.

I believe volumes have been written about educational ideals, yet we are in greater confusion than ever before. There is no method by which to educate a child to be integrated and free. As long as we are concerned with principles, ideals and methods, we are not helping the individual to be free from his own self-centered activity with all its fears and conflicts.

Ideals and blue-prints for a perfect Utopia will never bring about the radical change of heart which is essential if there is to be an end to war and universal destruction. Ideals cannot change our present values: they can be changed only by the right kind of education, which is to foster the understanding of what *is*.

When we are working together for an ideal, for the future, we shape individuals according to our conception of that future; we are not concerned with human beings at all, but with our idea of what they should be. The what *should be* becomes far more important to us than what *is*, namely, the individual with his complexities. If we begin to understand the individual directly instead of looking at him through the screen of what we think he should be, then we are concerned with what *is*. Then we no longer want to transform the individual into something else; our only concern is to help him to understand himself, and in this there is no personal motive or gain. If we are fully aware of what *is*, we shall understand it and so be free of it; but to be aware of what we are, we must stop struggling after something which we are not.

Ideals have no place in education for they prevent the comprehension of the present. Surely, we can be aware of what *is* only when we do not escape into the future. To look to the future, to strain after an ideal, indicates sluggishness of mind and a desire to avoid the present.

Is not the pursuit of a ready-made Utopia a denial of the freedom and integration of the individual? When one follows an ideal, a pattern, when one has a formula for what should be, does one not live a very superficial, automatic life? We need, not idealists or entities with mechanical minds, but integrated human beings who are intelligent and free. Merely to have a design for a perfect society is to wrangle and shed blood for what should be while ignoring what *is*.

If human beings were mechanical entities, automatic machines, then the future would be predictable and the plans for a perfect Utopia could be drawn up; then we would be able to plan carefully a future society and work towards it.

But human beings are not machines to be established according to a definite pattern.

Between now and the future there is an immense gap in which many influences are at work upon each one of us, and in sacrificing the present for the future we are pursuing wrong means to a probable right end. But the means determine the end; and besides, who are we to decide what man should be? By what right do we seek to mould him according to a particular pattern, learnt from some book or determined by our own ambitions, hopes and fears?

The right kind of education is not concerned with any ideology, however much it may promise a future Utopia: it is not based on any system, however carefully thought out; nor is it a means of conditioning the individual in some special manner. Education in the true sense is helping the individual to be mature and free, to flower greatly in love and goodness. That is what we should be interested in, and not in shaping the child according to some idealistic pattern.

Any method which classifies children according to temperament and aptitude merely emphasizes their differences; it breeds antagonism, encourages divisions in society and does not help to develop integrated human beings. It is obvious that no method or system can provide the right kind of education, and strict adherence to a particular method indicates sluggishness on the part of the educator. As long as education is based on cut-and-dried principles, it can turn out men and women who are efficient, but it cannot produce creative human beings.

Only love can bring about the understanding of another.

Where there is love there is instantaneous communion with the other, on the same level and at the same time. It is because we ourselves are so dry, empty and without love that we have allowed governments and systems to take over the education of our children and the direction of our lives; but governments want efficient technicians, not human beings, because human beings become dangerous to governments—and to organized religions as well. That is why governments and religious organizations seek to control education.

Life cannot be made to conform to a system, it cannot be forced into a framework, however nobly conceived; and a mind that has merely been trained in factual knowledge is incapable of meeting life with its variety, its subtlety, its depths and great heights. When we train our children according to a system of thought or a particular discipline, when we teach them to think within departmental divisions, we prevent them from growing into integrated men and women, and therefore they are incapable of thinking intelligently, which is to meet life as a whole.

The highest function of education is to bring about an integrated individual who is capable of dealing with life as a whole. The idealist, like the specialist, is not concerned with the whole, but only with a part. There can be no integration as long as one is pursuing an ideal pattern of action; and most teachers who are idealists have put away love, they have dry minds and hard hearts. To study a child, one has to be alert, watchful, self-aware, and this demands far greater intelligence and affection than to encourage him to follow an ideal.

The Right Kind of Education

Another function of education is to create new values. Merely to implant existing values in the mind of the child, to make him conform to ideals, is to condition him without awakening his intelligence. Education is intimately related to the present world crisis, and the educator who sees the causes of this universal chaos should ask himself how to awaken intelligence in the student, thus helping the coming generation not to bring about further conflict and disaster. He must give all his thought, all his care and affection to the creation of right environment and to the development of understanding, so that when the child grows into maturity he will be capable of dealing intelligently with the human problems that confront him. But in order to do this, the educator must understand himself instead of relying on ideologies, systems and beliefs.

Let us not think in terms of principles and ideals, but be concerned with things as they are; for it is the consideration of what *is* that awakens intelligence, and the intelligence of the educator is far more important than his knowledge of a new method of education. When one follows a method, even if it has been worked out by a thoughtful and intelligent person, the method becomes very important, and the children are important only as they fit into it. One measures and classifies the child, and then proceeds to educate him according to some chart. This process of education may be convenient for the teacher, but neither the practice of a system nor the tyranny of opinion and learning can bring about an integrated human being.

The right kind of education consists in understanding the

child as he is without imposing upon him an ideal of what we think he should be. To enclose him in the framework of an ideal is to encourage him to conform, which breeds fear and produces in him a constant conflict between what he is and what he should be; and all inward conflicts have their outward manifestations in society. Ideals are an actual hindrance to our understanding of the child and to the child's understanding of himself.

A parent who really desires to understand his child does not look at him through the screen of an ideal. If he loves the child, he observes him, he studies his tendencies, his moods and peculiarities. It is only when one feels no love for the child that one imposes upon him an ideal, for then one's ambitions are trying to fulfil themselves in him, wanting him to become this or that. If one loves, not the ideal, but the child, then there is a possibility of helping him to understand himself as he is.

If a child tells lies, for example, of what value is it to put before him the ideal of truth? One has to find out why he is telling lies. To help the child, one has to take time to study and observe him, which demands patience, love and care; but when one has no love, no understanding, then one forces the child into a pattern of action which we call an ideal.

Ideals are a convenient escape, and the teacher who follows them is incapable of understanding his students and dealing with them intelligently; for him, the future ideal, the what should be, is far more important than the present child. The pursuit of an ideal excludes love, and without love no human problem can be solved.

If the teacher is of the right kind, he will not depend on a method, but will study each individual pupil. In our relationship with children and young people, we are not dealing with mechanical devices that can be quickly repaired, but with living beings who are impressionable, volatile, sensitive, afraid, affectionate; and to deal with them, we have to have great understanding, the strength of patience and love. When we lack these, we look to quick and easy remedies and hope for marvellous and automatic results. If we are unaware, mechanical in our attitudes and actions, we fight shy of any demand upon us that is disturbing and that cannot be met by an automatic response, and this is one of our major difficulties in education.

The child is the result of both the past and the present and is therefore already conditioned. If we transmit our background to the child, we perpetuate both his and our own conditioning. There is radical transformation only when we understand our own conditioning and are free of it. To discuss what should be the right kind of education while we ourselves are conditioned is utterly futile.

While the children are young, we must of course protect them from physical harm and prevent them from feeling physically insecure. But unfortunately we do not stop there; we want to shape their ways of thinking and feeling, we want to mould them in accordance with our own cravings and intentions. We seek to fulfil ourselves in our children, to perpetuate ourselves through them. We build walls around them, condition them by our beliefs and ideologies, fears and hopes—and then we cry and pray when they are killed or maimed in wars, or otherwise made to suffer by the experiences of life.

Such experiences do not bring about freedom; on the contrary, they strengthen the will of the self. The self is made up of a series of defensive and expansive reactions, and its fulfilment is always in its own projections and gratifying identifications. As long as we translate experience in terms of the self, of the "me" and the "mine," as long as the "I," the ego, maintains itself through its reactions, experience cannot be freed from conflict, confusion and pain. Freedom comes only when one understands the ways of the self, the experiencer. It is only when the self, with its accumulated reactions, is not the experiencer, that experience takes on an entirely different significance and becomes creation.

If we would help the child to be free from the ways of the self, which cause so much suffering, then each one of us should set about altering deeply his attitude and relationship to the child. Parents and educators, by their own thought and conduct, can help the child to be free and to flower in love and goodness.

Education as it is at present in no way encourages the understanding of the inherited tendencies and environmental influences which condition the mind and heart and sustain fear, and therefore it does not help us to break through these conditionings and bring about an integrated human being. Any form of education that concerns itself with a part and not with the whole of man inevitably leads to increasing conflict and suffering.

It is only in individual freedom that love and goodness can flower; and the right kind of education alone can offer this freedom. Neither conformity to the present society nor the promise of a future Utopia can ever give to the individual that insight without which he is constantly creating problems.

The right kind of educator, seeing the inward nature of freedom, helps each individual student to observe and understand his own self-projected values and impositions; he helps him to become aware of the conditioning influences about him, and of his own desires, both of which limit his mind and breed fear; he helps him, as he grows to manhood, to observe and understand himself in relation to all things, for it is the craving for self-fulfilment that brings endless conflict and sorrow.

Surely, it is possible to help the individual to perceive the enduring values of life, without conditioning. Some may say that this full development of the individual will lead to chaos; but will it? There is already confusion in the world, and it has arisen because the individual has not been educated to understand himself. While he has been given some superficial freedom, he has also been taught to conform, to accept the existing values.

Against this regimentation, many are revolting; but unfortunately their revolt is a mere self-seeking reaction, which only further darkens our existence. The right kind of educator, aware of the mind's tendency to reaction, helps the student to alter present values, not out of reaction against them, but through understanding the total process of life. Full co-operation between man and man is not possible without the integration which right education can help to awaken in the individual.

Why are we so sure that neither we nor the coming generation, through the right kind of education, can bring about a fundamental alteration in human relationship? We have never tried it; and as most of us seem to be fearful of the right kind of education, we are disinclined to try it. Without really inquiring into this whole question, we assert that human nature cannot be changed, we accept things as they are and encourage the child to fit into the present society; we condition him to our present ways of life, and hope for the best. But can such conformity to present values, which lead to war and starvation, be considered education?

Let us not deceive ourselves that this conditioning is going to make for intelligence and happiness. If we remain fearful, devoid of affection, hopelessly apathetic, it means that we are really not interested in encouraging the individual to flower greatly in love and goodness, but prefer that he carry on the miseries with which we have burdened ourselves and of which he also is a part.

To condition the student to accept the present environment is quite obviously stupid. Unless we voluntarily bring about a radical change in education, we are directly responsible for the perpetuation of chaos and misery; and when some monstrous and brutal revolution finally comes, it will only give opportunity to another group of people to exploit and to be ruthless. Each group in power develops its own means of oppression, whether through psychological persuasion or brute force.

For political and industrial reasons, discipline has become an important factor in the present social structure, and it is because of our desire to be psychologically secure that we accept and practise various forms of discipline. Discipline guarantees a result, and to us the end is more important than the means; but the means determine the end.

One of the dangers of discipline is that the system becomes more important than the human beings who are enclosed in it. Discipline then becomes a substitute for love, and it is because our hearts are empty that we cling to discipline. Freedom can never come through discipline, through resistance; freedom is not a goal, an end to be achieved. Freedom is at the beginning, not at the end, it is not to be found in some distant ideal.

Freedom does not mean the opportunity for self-gratification or the setting aside of consideration for others. The teacher who is sincere will protect the children and help them in every possible way to grow towards the right kind of freedom; but it will be impossible for him to do this if he himself is addicted to an ideology, if he is in any way dogmatic or self-seeking.

Sensitivity can never be awakened through compulsion. One may compel a child to be outwardly quiet, but one has not come face to face with that which is making him obstinate, impudent, and so on. Compulsion breeds antagonism and fear. Reward and punishment in any form only make the mind subservient and dull; and if this is what we desire, then education through compulsion is an excellent way to proceed.

But such education cannot help us to understand the child, nor can it build a right social environment in which separatism and hatred will cease to exist. In the love of the child, right education is implied. But most of us do not love our children; we are ambitious for them—which means that we are ambitious for ourselves. Unfortunately, we are so busy with the occupations of the mind that we have little time for the promptings of the heart. After all, discipline implies resistance; and will resistance ever bring love? Discipline can only build walls about us; it is always exclusive, ever making for conflict. Discipline is not conducive to understanding; for understanding comes with observation, with inquiry in which all prejudice is set aside.

Discipline is an easy way to control a child, but it does not help him to understand the problems involved in living. Some form of compulsion, the discipline of punishment and reward, may be necessary to maintain order and seeming quietness among a large number of students herded together in a classroom; but with the right kind of educator and a small number of students, would any repression, politely called discipline, be required? If the classes are small and the teacher can give his full attention to each child, observing and helping him, then compulsion or domination in any form is obviously unnecessary. If, in such a group, a student persists in disorderliness or is unreasonably mischievous, the educator must inquire into the cause of his misbehaviour, which may be wrong diet, lack of rest, family wrangles, or some hidden fear.

Implicit in right education is the cultivation of freedom and intelligence, which is not possible if there is any form of compulsion, with its fears. After all, the concern of the educator is to help the student to understand the complexities of his whole being. To require him to suppress one part of his nature for the benefit of some other part is to create in him an endless conflict which results in social antagonisms. It is intelligence that brings order, not discipline.

Conformity and obedience have no place in the right kind of education. Co-operation between teacher and student is impossible if there is no mutual affection, mutual respect. When the showing of respect to elders is required of children, it generally becomes a habit, a mere outward performance, and fear assumes the form of veneration. Without respect and consideration, no vital relationship is possible, especially when the teacher is merely an instrument of his knowledge.

If the teacher demands respect from his pupils and has very little for them, it will obviously cause indifference and disrespect on their part. Without respect for human life, knowledge only leads to destruction and misery. The cultivation of respect for others is an essential part of right education, but if the educator himself has not this quality, he cannot help his students to an integrated life.

Intelligence is discernment of the essential, and to discern the essential there must be freedom from those hindrances which the mind projects in the search for its own security and comfort. Fear is inevitable as long as the mind is seeking security; and when human beings are regimented in any way, keen awareness and intelligence are destroyed.

The purpose of education is to cultivate right relationship, not only between individuals, but also between the individual and society; and that is why it is essential that education should, above all, help the individual to understand his own psychological process. Intelligence lies in understanding oneself and going above and beyond oneself; but there cannot be intelligence as long as there is fear. Fear perverts intelligence and is one of the causes of self-centered action. Discipline may suppress fear but does not eradicate it, and the superficial knowledge which we receive in modern education only further conceals it.

When we are young, fear is instilled into most of us both at home and at school. Neither parents nor teachers have the patience, the time or the wisdom to dispel the instinctive fears of childhood, which, as we grow up, dominate our attitudes and judgment and create a great many problems. The right kind of education must take into consideration this question of fear, because fear warps our whole outlook on life. To be without fear is the beginning of wisdom, and only the right kind of education can bring about the freedom from fear in which alone there is deep and creative intelligence.

Reward or punishment for any action merely strengthens self-centeredness. Action for the sake of another, in the name of the country or of God, leads to fear, and fear cannot be the basis for right action. If we would help a child to be considerate of others, we should not use love as a bribe, but take the time and have the patience to explain the ways of consideration.

There is no respect for another when there is a reward for it, for the bribe or the punishment becomes far more significant than the feeling of respect. If we have no respect for the child but merely offer him a reward or threaten him with punishment, we are encouraging acquisitiveness and fear. Because we ourselves have been brought up to act for the sake of a result, we do not see that there can be action free of the desire to gain.

The right kind of education will encourage thoughtfulness and consideration for others without enticements or threats of any kind. If we no longer seek immediate results, we shall begin to see how important it is that both the educator and the child should be free from the fear of punishment and the hope of reward, and from every other form of compulsion; but compulsion will continue as long as authority is part of relationship.

To follow authority has many advantages if one thinks in terms of personal motive and gain; but education based on individual advancement and profit can only build a social structure which is competitive, antagonistic and ruthless. This is the kind of society in which we have been brought up, and our animosity and confusion are obvious.

We have been taught to conform to the authority of a teacher, of a book, of a party, because it is profitable to do so. The specialists in every department of life, from the priest to the bureaucrat, wield authority and dominate us; but any government or teacher that uses compulsion can never bring about the co-operation in relationship which is essential for the welfare of society.

If we are to have right relationship between human beings, there should be no compulsion nor even persuasion. How can there be affection and genuine co-operation between those who are in power and those who are subject to power? By dispassionately considering this question of authority and its many implications, by seeing that the very desire for power is in itself destructive, there comes a spontaneous understanding of the whole process of authority. The moment we discard authority we are in partnership, and only then is there co-operation and affection.

The real problem in education is the educator. Even a small group of students becomes the instrument of his personal importance if he uses authority as a means of his own release, if teaching is for him a self-expansive fulfilment. But mere intellectual or verbal agreement concerning the crippling effects of authority is stupid and vain.

There must be deep insight into the hidden motivations of authority and domination. If we see that intelligence can never be awakened through compulsion, the very awareness of that fact will burn away our fears, and then we shall begin to cultivate a new environment which will be contrary to and far transcend the present social order.

To understand the significance of life with its conflicts and pain, we must think independently of any authority, including the authority of organized religion; but if in our desire to help the child we set before him authoritative examples, we shall only be encouraging fear, imitation and various forms of superstition.

Those who are religiously inclined try to impose upon the child the beliefs, hopes and fears which they in turn have acquired from their parents; and those who are anti-religious are equally keen to influence the child to accept the particular way of thinking which they happen to follow. We all want our children to accept our form of worship or take to heart our chosen ideology. It is so easy to get entangled in images and formulations, whether invented by ourselves or by others, and therefore it is necessary to be ever watchful and alert.

What we call religion is merely organized belief, with its dogmas, rituals, mysteries and superstitions. Each religion has its own sacred book, its mediator, its priests and its ways of threatening and holding people. Most of us have been conditioned to all this, which is considered religious education; but this conditioning sets man against man, it creates antagonism, not only among the believers, but also against those of other beliefs. Though all religions assert that they worship God and say that we must love one another, they instill fear through their doctrines of reward and punishment, and through their competitive dogmas they perpetuate suspicion and antagonism.

Dogmas, mysteries and rituals are not conducive to a spiritual life. Religious education in the true sense is to encourage the child to understand his own relationship to people, to things and to nature. There is no existence without

37

relationship; and without self-knowledge, all relationship, with the one and with the many, brings conflict and sorrow. Of course, to explain this fully to a child is impossible; but if the educator and the parents deeply grasp the full significance of relationship, then by their attitude, conduct and speech they will surely be able to convey to the child, without too many words and explanations, the meaning of a spiritual life.

Our so-called religious training discourages questioning and doubt, yet it is only when we inquire into the significance of the values which society and religion have placed about us that we begin to find out what is true. It is the function of the educator to examine deeply his own thoughts and feelings and to put aside those values which have given him security and comfort, for only then can he help his students to be self-aware and to understand their own urges and fears.

The time to grow straight and clear is when one is young; and those of us who are older can, if we have understanding, help the young to free themselves from the hindrances which society has imposed upon them, as well as from those which they themselves are projecting. If the child's mind and heart are not moulded by religious preconceptions and prejudices, then he will be free to discover through self-knowledge what is above and beyond himself.

True religion is not a set of beliefs and rituals, hopes and fears; and if we can allow the child to grow up without these hindering influences, then perhaps, as he matures, he will begin to inquire into the nature of reality, of God.

That is why, in educating a child, deep insight and understanding are necessary.

Most people who are religiously inclined, who talk about God and immortality, do not fundamentally believe in individual freedom and integration; yet religion is the cultivation of freedom in the search for truth. There can be no compromise with freedom. Partial freedom for the individual is no freedom at all. Conditioning of any kind, whether political or religious, is not freedom and it will never bring peace.

Religion is not a form of conditioning. It is a state of tranquillity in which there is reality, God; but that creative state can come into being only when there is self-knowledge and freedom. Freedom brings virtue, and without virtue there can be no tranquillity. The still mind is not a conditioned mind, it is not disciplined or trained to be still. Stillness comes only when the mind understands its own ways, which are the ways of the self.

Organized religion is the frozen thought of man, out of which he builds temples and churches; it has become a solace for the fearful, an opiate for those who are in sorrow. But God or truth is far beyond thought and emotional demands. Parents and teachers who recognize the psychological processes which build up fear and sorrow should be able to help the young to observe and understand their own conflicts and trials.

If we who are older can help the children, as they grow up, to think clearly and dispassionately, to love and not to breed animosity, what more is there to do? But if we are constantly at one another's throats, if we are incapable of bringing about order and peace in the world by deeply changing ourselves, of what value are the sacred books and the myths of the various religions?

True religious education is to help the child to be intelligently aware, to discern for himself the temporary and the real, and to have a disinterested approach to life; and would it not have more meaning to begin each day at home or at school with a serious thought, or with a reading that has depth and significance, rather than mumble some oft-repeated words or phrases?

Past generations, with their ambitions, traditions and ideals, have brought misery and destruction to the world; perhaps the coming generations, with the right kind of education, can put an end to this chaos and build a happier social order. If those who are young have the spirit of inquiry, if they are constantly searching out the truth of all things, political and religious, personal and environmental, then youth will have great significance and there is hope for a better world.

Most children are curious, they want to know; but their eager inquiry is dulled by our pontifical assertions, our superior impatience and our casual brushing aside of their curiosity. We do not encourage their inquiry, for we are rather apprehensive of what may be asked of us; we do not foster their discontent, for we ourselves have ceased to question.

Most parents and teachers are afraid of discontent because it is disturbing to all forms of security, and so they encourage the young to overcome it through safe jobs, inheritance, marriage and the consolation of religious dogmas. Elders, knowing only too well the many ways of blunting the mind and the heart, proceed to make the child as dull as they are by impressing upon him the authorities, traditions and beliefs which they themselves have accepted.

Only by encouraging the child to question the book, whatever it be, to inquire into the validity of the existing social values, traditions, forms of government, religious beliefs and so on, can the educator and the parents hope to awaken and sustain his critical alertness and keen insight.

The young, if they are at all alive, are full of hope and discontent; they must be, otherwise they are already old and dead. And the old are those who were once discontented, but who have successfully smothered that flame and have found security and comfort in various ways. They crave permanency for themselves and their families, they ardently desire certainty in ideas, in relationships, in possessions; so the moment they feel discontented, they become absorbed in their responsibilities, in their jobs, or in anything else, in order to escape from that disturbing feeling of discontent.

While we are young is the time to be discontented, not only with ourselves, but also with the things about us. We should learn to think clearly and without bias, so as not to be inwardly dependent and fearful. Independence is not for that coloured section of the map which we call our country, but for ourselves as individuals; and though outwardly we are dependent on one another, this mutual dependence does not become cruel or oppressive if inwardly we are free of the craving for power, position and authority.

We must understand discontent, of which most of us are afraid. Discontent may bring what appears to be disorder; but if it leads, as it should, to self-knowledge and self-abnegation, then it will create a new social order and enduring peace. With self-abnegation comes immeasurable joy.

Discontent is the means to freedom; but in order to inquire without bias, there must be none of the emotional dissipation which often takes the form of political gatherings, the shouting of slogans, the search for a *guru* or spiritual teacher, and religious orgies of different kinds. This dissipation dulls the mind and heart, making them incapable of insight and therefore easily moulded by circumstances and fear. It is the burning desire to inquire, and not the easy imitation of the multitude, that will bring about a new understanding of the ways of life.

The young are so easily persuaded by the priest or the politician, by the rich or the poor, to think in a particular way; but the right kind of education should help them to be watchful of these influences so that they do not repeat slogans like parrots or fall into any cunning trap of greed, whether their own or that of another. They must not allow authority to stifle their minds and hearts. To follow another, however great, or to give one's adherence to a gratifying ideology, will not bring about a peaceful world.

When we leave school or college, many of us put away books and seem to feel that we are done with learning;

and there are those who are stimulated to think further afield, who keep on reading and absorbing what others have said, and become addicted to knowledge. As long as there is the worship of knowledge or technique as a means to success and dominance, there must be ruthless competition, antagonism and the ceaseless struggle for bread.

As long as success is our goal we cannot be rid of fear, for the desire to succeed inevitably breeds the fear of failure. That is why the young should not be taught to worship success. Most people seek success in one form or another, whether on the tennis court, in the business world, or in politics. We all want to be on top, and this desire creates constant conflict within ourselves and with our neighbours; it leads to competition, envy, animosity and finally to war.

Like the older generation, the young also seek success and security; though at first they may be discontented, they soon become respectable and are afraid to say no to society. The walls of their own desires begin to enclose them, and they fall in line and assume the reins of authority. Their discontent, which is the very flame of inquiry, of search, of understanding, grows dull and dies away, and in its place there comes the desire for a better job, a rich marriage, a successful career, all of which is the craving for more security.

There is no essential difference between the old and the young, for both are slaves to their own desires and gratifications. Maturity is not a matter of age, it comes with understanding. The ardent spirit of inquiry is perhaps easier for the young, because those who are older have been battered about by life, conflicts have worn them out and death in different forms awaits them. This does not mean that they are incapable of purposive inquiry, but only that it is more difficult for them.

Many adults are immature and rather childish, and this is a contributing cause of the confusion and misery in the world. It is the older people who are responsible for the prevailing economic and moral crisis; and one of our unfortunate weaknesses is that we want someone else to act for us and change the course of our lives. We wait for others to revolt and build anew, and we remain inactive until we are assured of the outcome.

It is security and success that most of us are after; and a mind that is seeking security, that craves success, is not intelligent, and is therefore incapable of integrated action. There can be integrated action only if one is aware of one's own conditioning, of one's racial, national, political and religious prejudices; that is, only if one realizes that the ways of the self are ever separative.

Life is a well of deep waters. One can come to it with small buckets and draw only a little water, or one can come with large vessels, drawing plentiful waters that will nourish and sustain. While one is young is the time to investigate, to experiment with everything. The school should help its young people to discover their vocations and responsibilities, and not merely cram their minds with facts and technical knowledge; it should be the soil in which they can grow without fear, happily and integrally.

The Right Kind of Education

To educate a child is to help him to understand freedom and integration. To have freedom there must be order, which virtue alone can give; and integration can take place only when there is great simplicity. From innumerable complexities we must grow to simplicity; we must become simple in our inward life and in our outward needs.

Education is at present concerned with outward efficiency, and it utterly disregards, or deliberately perverts, the inward nature of man; it develops only one part of him and leaves the rest to drag along as best it can. Our inner confusion, antagonism and fear ever overcome the outer structure of society, however nobly conceived and cunningly built. When there is not the right kind of education we destroy one another, and physical security for every individual is denied. To educate the student rightly is to help him to understand the total process of himself; for it is only when there is integration of the mind and heart in everyday action that there can be intelligence and inward transformation.

While offering information and technical training, education should above all encourage an integrated outlook on life; it should help the student to recognize and break down in himself all social distinctions and prejudices, and discourage the acquisitive pursuit of power and domination. It should encourage the right kind of self-observation and the experiencing of life as a whole, which is not to give significance to the part, to the "me" and the "mine," but to help the mind to go above and beyond itself to discover the real.

Freedom comes into being only through self-knowledge in one's daily occupations, that is, in one's relationship with people, with things, with ideas and with nature. If the educator is helping the student to be integrated, there can be no fanatical or unreasonable emphasis on any particular phase of life. It is the understanding of the total process of existence that brings integration. When there is self-knowledge, the power of creating illusions ceases, and only then is it possible for reality or God to be.

Human beings must be integrated if they are to come out of any crisis, and especially the present world crisis, without being broken; therefore, to parents and teachers who are really interested in education, the main problem is how to develop an integrated individual. To do this, the educator himself must obviously be integrated; so the right kind of education is of the highest importance, not only for the young, but also for the older generation if they are willing to learn and are not too set in their ways. What we are in ourselves is much more important than the traditional question of what to teach the child, and if we love our children we will see to it that they have the right kind of educators.

Teaching should not become a specialist's profession. When it does, as is so often the case, love fades away; and love is essential to the process of integration. To be integrated there must be freedom from fear. Fearlessness brings independence without ruthlessness, without contempt for another, and this is the most essential factor in life. Without love we cannot work out our many conflicting problems; without love the acquisition of knowledge only increases confusion and leads to self-destruction.

The integrated human being will come to technique through experiencing, for the creative impulse makes its own technique—and that is the greatest art. When a child has the creative impulse to paint, he paints, he does not bother about technique. Likewise people who are experiencing, and *therefore* teaching, are the only real teachers, and they too will create their own technique.

This sounds very simple, but it is really a deep revolution. If we think about it we can see the extraordinary effect it will have on society. At present most of us are washed out at the age of forty-five or fifty by slavery to routine; through compliance, through fear and acceptance, we are finished, though we struggle on in a society that has very little meaning except for those who dominate it and are secure. If the teacher sees this and is himself really experiencing, then whatever his temperament and capacities may be, his teaching will not be a matter of routine but will become an instrument of help.

To understand a child we have to watch him at play, study him in his different moods; we cannot project upon him our own prejudices, hopes and fears, or mould him to fit the pattern of our desires. If we are constantly judging the child according to our personal likes and dislikes, we are bound to create barriers and hindrances in our relationship with him and in his relationships with the world. Unfortunately, most of us desire to shape the child in a way that is gratifying to our own vanities and idiosyncrasies; we find varying degrees of comfort and satisfaction in exclusive ownership and domination.

Surely, this process is not relationship, but mere imposition, and it is therefore essential to understand the difficult and complex desire to dominate. It takes many subtle forms; and in its self-righteous aspect, it is very obstinate. The desire to "serve" with the unconscious longing to dominate is difficult to understand. Can there be love where there is possessiveness? Can we be in communion with those whom we seek to control? To dominate is to use another for self-gratification, and where there is the use of another there is no love.

When there is love there is consideration, not only for the children but for every human being. Unless we are deeply touched by the problem, we will never find the right way of education. Mere technical training inevitably makes for ruthlessness, and to educate our children we must be sensitive to the whole movement of life. What we think, what we do, what we say matters infinitely, because it creates the environment, and the environment either helps or hinders the child.

Obviously, then, those of us who are deeply interested in this problem will have to begin to understand ourselves and thereby help to transform society; we will make it our direct responsibility to bring about a new approach to education. If we love our children, will we not find a way of putting an end to war? But if we are merely using the word "love" without substance, then the whole complex problem of human misery will remain. The way out of this problem lies through ourselves. We must begin to understand our relationship with our fellow-men, with nature, with ideas and with things, for without that understanding there is no hope, there is no way out of conflict and suffering.

The bringing up of a child requires intelligent observation and care. Experts and their knowledge can never replace the parents' love, but most parents corrupt that love by their own fears and ambitions, which condition and distort the outlook of the child. So few of us are concerned with love, but we are vastly taken up with the appearance of love.

The present educational and social structure does not help the individual towards freedom and integration; and if the parents are at all in earnest and desire that the child shall grow to his fullest integral capacity, they must begin to alter the influence of the home and set about creating schools with the right kind of educators.

The influence of the home and that of the school must not be in any way contradictory, so both parents and teachers must re-educate themselves. The contradiction which so often exists between the private life of the individual and his life as a member of the group creates an endless battle within himself and in his relationships.

This conflict is encouraged and sustained through the wrong kind of education, and both governments and organized religions add to the confusion by their contradictory doctrines. The child is divided within himself from the very start, which results in personal and social disasters.

If those of us who love our children and see the urgency of this problem will set our minds and hearts to it, then, however few we may be, through right education and an intelligent home environment, we can help to bring about integrated human beings; but if, like so many others, we fill our hearts with the cunning things of the mind, then we shall continue to see our children destroyed in wars, in famines, and by their own psychological conflicts.

Right education comes with the transformation of ourselves. We must re-educate ourselves not to kill one another for any cause, however righteous, for any ideology, however promising it may appear to be for the future happiness of the world. We must learn to be compassionate, to be content with little, and to seek the Supreme, for only then can there be the true salvation of mankind.

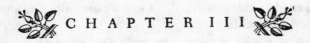

CHAPTER III

INTELLECT, AUTHORITY
AND INTELLIGENCE

MANY of us seem to think that by teaching every human being to read and write, we shall solve our human problems; but this idea has proved to be false. The so-called educated are not peace-loving, integrated people, and they too are responsible for the confusion and misery of the world.

The right kind of education means the awakening of intelligence, the fostering of an integrated life, and only such education can create a new culture and a peaceful world; but to bring about this new kind of education, we must make a fresh start on an entirely different basis.

With the world falling into ruin about us, we discuss theories and vain political questions, and play with superficial reforms. Does this not indicate utter thoughtlessness on our part? Some may agree that it does, but they will go on doing exactly as they have always done—and that is the sadness of existence. When we hear a truth and do not act upon it, it becomes a poison within ourselves, and that poison spreads, bringing psychological disturbances, un-balance and ill-health. Only when creative intelligence is awakened in the individual is there a possibility of a peaceful and happy life.

We cannot be intelligent by merely substituting one government for another, one party or class for another, one exploiter for another. Bloody revolution can never solve our problems. Only a profound inward revolution which alters all our values can create a different environment, an intelligent social structure, and such a revolution can be brought about only by you and me. No new order will arise until we individually break down our own psychological barriers and are free.

On paper we can draw the blue-prints for a brilliant Utopia, a brave new world; but the sacrifice of the present to an unknown future will certainly never solve any of our problems. There are so many elements intervening between now and the future, that no man can know what the future will be. What we can and must do if we are in earnest, is to tackle our problems now, and not postpone them to the future. Eternity is not in the future; eternity is now. Our problems exist in the present, and it is only in the present that they can be solved.

Those of us who are serious must regenerate ourselves; but there can be regeneration only when we break away from those values which we have created through our self-protective and aggressive desires. Self-knowledge is the beginning of freedom, and it is only when we know ourselves that we can bring about order and peace.

Now, some may ask, "What can a single individual do that will affect history? Can he accomplish anything at all by the way he lives?" Certainly he can. You and I are obviously not going to stop the immediate wars, or create an instantaneous understanding between nations; but at least we can bring about, in the world of our everyday relationships, a fundamental change which will have its own effect.

Individual enlightenment does affect large groups of people, but only if one is not eager for results. If one thinks in terms of gain and effect, right transformation of oneself is not possible.

Human problems are not simple, they are very complex. To understand them requires patience and insight, and it is of the highest importance that we as individuals understand and resolve them for ourselves. They are not to be understood through easy formulas or slogans; nor can they be solved at their own level by specialists working along a particular line, which only leads to further confusion and misery. Our many problems can be understood and resolved only when we are aware of ourselves as a total process, that is, when we understand our whole psychological make-up; and no religious or political leader can give us the key to that understanding.

To understand ourselves, we must be aware of our relationship, not only with people, but also with property, with ideas and with nature. If we are to bring about a true revolution in human relationship, which is the basis of all society, there must be a fundamental change in our own

53

values and outlook; but we avoid the necessary and fundamental transformation of ourselves, and try to bring about
political revolutions in the world, which always leads to
bloodshed and disaster.

Relationship based on sensation can never be a means of
release from the self; yet most of our relationships are
based on sensation, they are the outcome of our desire for
personal advantage, for comfort, for psychological security.
Though they may offer us a momentary escape from the
self, such relationships only give strength to the self, with its
enclosing and binding activities. Relationship is a mirror
in which the self and all its activities can be seen; and it is
only when the ways of the self are understood in the
reactions of relationship that there is creative release from
the self.

To transform the world, there must be regeneration
within ourselves. Nothing can be achieved by violence, by
the easy liquidation of one another. We may find a temporary release by joining groups, by studying methods of social
and economic reform, by enacting legislation, or by praying;
but do what we will, without self-knowledge and the love
that is inherent in it, our problems will ever expand and
multiply. Whereas, if we apply our minds and hearts to the
task of knowing ourselves, we shall undoubtedly solve our
many conflicts and sorrows.

Modern education is making us into thoughtless entities; it does very little towards helping us to find our
individual vocation. We pass certain examinations and then,
with luck, we get a job—which often means endless routine

for the rest of our life. We may dislike our job, but we are forced to continue with it because we have no other means of livelihood. We may want to do something entirely different, but commitments and responsibilities hold us down, and we are hedged in by our own anxieties and fears. Being frustrated, we seek escape through sex, drink, politics or fanciful religion.

When our ambitions are thwarted, we give undue importance to that which should be normal, and we develop a psychological twist. Until we have a comprehensive understanding of our life and love, of our political, religious and social desires, with their demands and hindrances, we shall have ever-increasing problems in our relationships, leading us to misery and destruction.

Ignorance is lack of knowledge of the ways of the self, and this ignorance cannot be dissipated by superficial activities and reforms; it can be dissipated only by one's constant awareness of the movements and responses of the self in all its relationships.

What we must realize is that we are not only conditioned by environment, but that we *are* the environment—we are not something apart from it. Our thoughts and responses are conditioned by the values which society, of which we are a part, has imposed upon us.

We never see that we are the total environment because there are several entities in us, all revolving around the "me," the self. The self is made up of these entities, which are merely desires in various forms. From this conglomeration of desires arises the central figure, the thinker, the will of the "me" and the "mine"; and a division is thus established between the self and the not-self, between the "me" and the environment or society. This separation is the beginning of conflict, inward and outward.

Awareness of this whole process, both the conscious and the hidden, is meditation; and through this meditation the self, with its desires and conflicts, is transcended. Self-knowledge is necessary if one is to be free of the influences and values that give shelter to the self; and in this freedom alone is there creation, truth, God, or what you will.

Opinion and tradition mould our thoughts and feelings from the tenderest age. The immediate influences and impressions produce an effect which is powerful and lasting, and which shapes the whole course of our conscious and unconscious life. Conformity begins in childhood through education and the impact of society.

The desire to imitate is a very strong factor in our life, not only at the superficial levels, but also profoundly. We have hardly any independent thoughts and feelings. When they do occur, they are mere reactions, and are therefore not free from the established pattern; for there is no freedom in reaction.

Philosophy and religion lay down certain methods whereby we can come to the realization of truth or God; yet merely to follow a method is to remain thoughtless and unintegrated, however beneficial the method may seem to be in our daily social life. The urge to conform, which is the desire for security, breeds fear and brings to the fore the political and religious authorities, the leaders and heroes who encourage subservience and by whom we are subtly or grossly dominated; but *not* to conform is only a reaction against authority, and in no way helps us to become integrated human beings. Reaction is endless, it only leads to further reaction.

Conformity, with its undercurrent of fear, is a hindrance; but mere intellectual recognition of this fact will not resolve the hindrance. It is only when we are aware of hindrances with our whole being that we can be free of them without creating further and deeper blockages.

When we are inwardly dependent, then tradition has a great hold on us; and a mind that thinks along traditional lines cannot discover that which is new. By conforming we become mediocre imitators, cogs in a cruel social machine. It is what *we* think that matters, not what others *want* us to think. When we conform to tradition, we soon become mere copies of what we should be.

This imitation of what we should be, breeds fear; and fear kills creative thinking. Fear dulls the mind and heart so that we are not alert to the whole significance of life; we become insensitive to our own sorrows, to the movement of the birds, to the smiles and miseries of others.

Conscious and unconscious fear has many different causes, and it needs alert watchfulness to be rid of them all. Fear cannot be eliminated through discipline, sublimation, or through any other act of will: its causes have to be searched out and understood. This needs patience and an awareness in which there is no judgment of any kind.

It is comparatively easy to understand and dissolve our

conscious fears. But unconscious fears are not even discovered by most of us, for we do not allow them to come to the surface; and when on rare occasions they do come to the surface, we hasten to cover them up, to escape from them. Hidden fears often make their presence known through dreams and other forms of intimation, and they cause greater deterioration and conflict than do the superficial fears.

Our lives are not just on the surface, their greater part is concealed from casual observation. If we would have our obscure fears come into the open and dissolve, the conscious mind must be somewhat still, not everlastingly occupied; then, as these fears come to the surface, they must be observed without let or hindrance, for any form of condemnation or justification only strengthens fear. To be free from all fear, we must be awake to its darkening influence, and only constant watchfulness can reveal its many causes.

One of the results of fear is the acceptance of authority in human affairs. Authority is created by our desire to be right, to be secure, to be comfortable, to have no conscious conflicts or disturbances; but nothing which results from fear can help us to understand our problems, even though fear may take the form of respect and submission to the so-called wise. The wise wield no authority, and those in authority are not wise. Fear in whatever form prevents the understanding of ourselves and of our relationship to all things.

The following of authority is the denial of intelligence. To accept authority is to submit to domination, to subjugate oneself to an individual, to a group, or to an ideology, whether religious or political; and this subjugation of oneself to authority is the denial, not only of intelligence, but also of individual freedom. Compliance with a creed or a system of ideas is a self-protective reaction. The acceptance of authority may help us temporarily to cover up our difficulties and problems; but to avoid a problem is only to intensify it, and in the process, self-knowledge and freedom are abandoned.

How can there be compromise between freedom and the acceptance of authority? If there *is* compromise, then those who say they are seeking self-knowledge and freedom are not earnest in their endeavor. We seem to think that freedom is an ultimate end, a goal, and that in order to become free we must first submit ourselves to various forms of suppression and intimidation. We hope to achieve freedom through conformity; but are not the means as important as the end? Do not the means shape the end?

To have peace, one must employ peaceful means; for if the means are violent, how can the end be peaceful? If the end is freedom, the beginning must be free, for the end and the beginning are one. There can be self-knowledge and intelligence only when there is freedom at the very outset; and freedom is denied by the acceptance of authority.

We worship authority in various forms: knowledge, success, power, and so on. We exert authority on the young, and at the same time we are afraid of superior authority. When man himself has no inward vision, outward power and position assume vast importance, and then the individual is more and more subject to authority and compulsion, he becomes the instrument of others. We can see this process going on around us: in moments of crisis, the democratic nations act like the totalitarian, forgetting their democracy and forcing man to conform.

If we can understand the compulsion behind our desire to dominate or to be dominated, then perhaps we can be free from the crippling effects of authority. We crave to be certain, to be right, to be successful, to know; and this desire for certainty, for permanence, builds up within ourselves the authority of personal experience, while outwardly it creates the authority of society, of the family, of religion, and so on. But merely to ignore authority, to shake off its outward symbols, is of very little significance.

To break away from one tradition and conform to another, to leave this leader and follow that, is but a superficial gesture. If we are to be aware of the whole process of authority, if we are to see the inwardness of it, if we are to understand and transcend the desire for certainty, then we must have extensive awareness and insight, we must be free, not at the end, but at the beginning.

The craving for certainty, for security is one of the major activities of the self, and it is this compelling urge that has to be constantly watched, and not merely twisted or forced in another direction, or made to conform to a desired pattern. The self, the "me" and the "mine," is very strong in most of us; sleeping or waking, it is ever alert, always strengthening itself. But when there is an awareness of the self and a realization that all its activities, however subtle, must inevitably lead to conflict and pain, then the craving for certainty, for self-continuance comes to an end. One has to be constantly watchful for the self to reveal its ways and tricks; but when we begin to understand them, and to understand the implications of authority and all that is involved in our acceptance and denial of it, then we are already disentangling ourselves from authority.

As long as the mind allows itself to be dominated and controlled by the desire for its own security, there can be no release from the self and its problems; and that is why there is no release from the self through dogma and organized belief, which we call religion. Dogma and belief are only projections of our own mind. The rituals, the *puja*, the accepted forms of meditation, the constantly-repeated words and phrases, though they may produce certain gratifying responses, do not free the mind from the self and its activities; for the self is essentially the outcome of sensation.

In moments of sorrow, we turn to what we call God, which is but an image of our own minds; or we find gratifying explanations, and this gives us temporary comfort. The religions that we follow are created by our hopes and fears, by our desire for inward security and reassurance; and with the worship of authority, whether it is that of a saviour, a master or a priest, there come submission, acceptance and imitation. So, we are exploited in the name of God, as we are exploited in the name of parties and ideologies—and we go on suffering.

We are all human beings, by whatever name we may call ourselves, and suffering is our lot. Sorrow is common to all

61

of us, to the idealist and to the materialist. Idealism is an escape from what *is*, and materialism is another way of denying the measureless depths of the present. Both the idealist and the materialist have their own ways of avoiding the complex problem of suffering; both are consumed by their own cravings, ambitions and conflicts, and their ways of life are not conducive to tranquillity. They are both responsible for the confusion and misery of the world.

Now, when we are in a state of conflict, of suffering, there is no comprehension: in that state, however cunningly and carefully thought out our action may be, it can only lead to further confusion and sorrow. To understand conflict and so to be free from it, there must be an awareness of the ways of the conscious and of the unconscious mind.

No idealism, no system or pattern of any kind, can help us to unravel the deep workings of the mind; on the contrary, any formulation or conclusion will hinder their discovery. The pursuit of what should be, the attachment to principles, to ideals, the establishment of a goal—all this leads to many illusions. If we are to know ourselves, there must be a certain spontaneity, a freedom to observe, and this is not possible when the mind is enclosed in the superficial, in idealistic or materialistic values.

Existence is relationship; and whether we belong to an organized religion or not, whether we are worldly or caught up in ideals, our suffering can be resolved only through the understanding of ourselves in relationship. Self-knowledge alone can bring tranquillity and happiness to man, for self-knowledge is the beginning of intelligence and integration. Intelligence is not mere superficial adjustment; it is not the cultivation of the mind, the acquisition of knowledge. Intelligence is the capacity to understand the ways of life, it is the perception of right values.

Modern education, in developing the intellect, offers more and more theories and facts, without bringing about the understanding of the total process of human existence. We are highly intellectual; we have developed cunning minds, and are caught up in explanations. The intellect is satisfied with theories and explanations, but intelligence is not; and for the understanding of the total process of existence, there must be an integration of the mind and heart in action. Intelligence is not separate from love.

For most of us, to accomplish this inward revolution is extremely arduous. We know how to meditate, how to play the piano, how to write, but we have no knowledge of the meditator, the player, the writer. We are not creators, for we have filled our hearts and minds with knowledge, information and arrogance; we are full of quotations from what others have thought or said. But experiencing comes first, not the way of experiencing. There must be love before there can be the expression of love.

It is clear, then, that merely to cultivate the intellect, which is to develop capacity or knowledge, does not result in intelligence. There is a distinction between intellect and intelligence. Intellect is thought functioning independently of emotion, whereas, intelligence is the capacity to feel as well as to reason; and until we approach life with intelligence, instead of intellect alone, or with emotion alone, no political or educational system in the world can save us from the toils of chaos and destruction.

Knowledge is not comparable with intelligence, knowledge is not wisdom. Wisdom is not marketable, it is not a merchandise that can be bought with the price of learning or discipline. Wisdom cannot be found in books; it cannot be accumulated, memorized or stored up. Wisdom comes with the abnegation of the self. To have an open mind is more important than learning; and we can have an open mind, not by cramming it full of information, but by being aware of our own thoughts and feelings, by carefully observing ourselves and the influences about us, by listening to others, by watching the rich and the poor, the powerful and the lowly. Wisdom does not come through fear and oppression, but through the observation and understanding of everyday incidents in human relationship.

In our search for knowledge, in our acquisitive desires, we are losing love, we are blunting the feeling for beauty, the sensitivity to cruelty; we are becoming more and more specialized and less and less integrated. Wisdom cannot be replaced by knowledge, and no amount of explanation, no accumulation of facts, will free man from suffering. Knowledge is necessary, science has its place; but if the mind and heart are suffocated by knowledge, and if the cause of suffering is explained away, life becomes vain and meaningless. And is this not what is happening to most of us? Our education is making us more and more shallow; it is not helping us to uncover the deeper layers of our being, and our lives are increasingly disharmonious and empty.

Information, the knowledge of facts, though ever increasing, is by its very nature limited. Wisdom is infinite, it includes knowledge and the way of action; but we take hold of a branch and think it is the whole tree. Through the knowledge of the part, we can never realize the joy of the whole. Intellect can never lead to the whole, for it is only a segment, a part.

We have separated intellect from feeling, and have developed intellect at the expense of feeling. We are like a three-legged object with one leg much longer than the others, and we have no balance. We are trained to be intellectual; our education cultivates the intellect to be sharp, cunning, acquisitive, and so it plays the most important rôle in our life. Intelligence is much greater than intellect, for it is the integration of reason and love; but there can be intelligence only when there is self-knowledge, the deep understanding of the total process of oneself.

What is essential for man, whether young or old, is to live fully, integrally, and that is why our major problem is the cultivation of that intelligence which brings integration. Undue emphasis on any part of our total make-up gives a partial and therefore distorted view of life, and it is this distortion which is causing most of our difficulties. Any partial development of our whole temperament is bound to be disastrous both for ourselves and for society, and so it is really very important that we approach our human problems with an integrated point of view.

To be an integrated human being is to understand the entire process of one's own consciousness, both the hidden and the open. This is not possible if we give undue emphasis to the intellect. We attach great importance to the cultivation of the mind, but inwardly we are insufficient, poor and confused. This living in the intellect is the way of disintegration; for ideas, like beliefs, can never bring people together except in conflicting groups.

As long as we depend on thought as a means of integration, there must be disintegration; and to understand the disintegrating action of thought is to be aware of the ways of the self, the ways of one's own desire. We must be aware of our conditioning and its responses, both collective and personal. It is only when one is fully aware of the activities of the self with its contradictory desires and pursuits, its hopes and fears, that there is a possibility of going beyond the self.

Only love and right thinking will bring about true revolution, the revolution within ourselves. But how are we to have love? Not through the pursuit of the ideal of love, but only when there is no hatred, when there is no greed, when the sense of self, which is the cause of antagonism, comes to an end. A man who is caught up in the pursuits of exploitation, of greed, of envy, can never love.

Without love and right thinking, oppression and cruelty will ever be on the increase. The problem of man's antagonism to man can be solved, not by pursuing the ideal of peace, but by understanding the causes of war which lie in our attitude towards life, towards our fellow-beings; and this understanding can come about only through the right kind of education. Without a change of heart, without goodwill, without the inward transformation which is born of self-awareness, there can be no peace, no happiness for men.

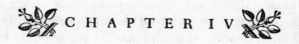

CHAPTER IV

EDUCATION AND WORLD PEACE

TO DISCOVER what part education can play in the present world crisis, we should understand how that crisis has come into being. It is obviously the result of wrong values in our relationship to people, to property and to ideas. If our relationship with others is based on self-aggrandizement, and our relationship to property is acquisitive, the structure of society is bound to be competitive and self-isolating. If in our relationship with ideas we justify one ideology in opposition to another, mutual distrust and ill-will are the inevitable results.

Another cause of the present chaos is dependence on authority, on leaders, whether in daily life, in the small school or in the university. Leaders and their authority are deteriorating factors in any culture. When we follow another there is no understanding, but only fear and conformity, eventually leading to the cruelty of the totalitarian State and the dogmatism of organized religion.

To rely on governments, to look to organizations and authorities for that peace which must begin with the understanding of ourselves, is to create further and still greater conflict; and there can be no lasting happiness as long as we accept a social order in which there is endless strife and antagonism between man and man. If we want to change existing conditions, we must first transform ourselves, which means that we must become aware of our own actions, thoughts and feelings in everyday life.

But we do not really want peace, we do not want to put an end to exploitation. We will not allow our greed to be interfered with, or the foundations of our present social structure to be altered; we want things to continue as they are with only superficial modifications, and so the powerful, the cunning inevitably rule our lives.

Peace is not achieved through any ideology, it does not depend on legislation; it comes only when we as individuals begin to understand our own psychological process. If we avoid the responsibility of acting individually and wait for some new system to establish peace, we shall merely become the slaves of that system.

When governments, dictators, big business and the clerically powerful begin to see that this increasing antagonism between men only leads to indiscriminate destruction and is therefore no longer profitable, they may force us, through legislation and other means of compulsion, to suppress our personal cravings and ambitions and to co-operate for the well-being of mankind. Just as we are now educated and encouraged to be competitive and ruthless, so then we shall be compelled to respect one another and to work for the world as a whole.

And even though we may all be well fed, clothed and sheltered, we shall not be free of our conflicts and antagonisms, which will merely have shifted to another plane, where they will be still more diabolical and devastating. The only moral or righteous action is voluntary, and understanding alone can bring peace and happiness to man.

Beliefs, ideologies and organized religions are setting us against our neighbours; there is conflict, not only among different societies, but among groups within the same society. We must realize that as long as we identify ourselves with a country, as long as we cling to security, as long as we are conditioned by dogmas, there will be strife and misery both within ourselves and in the world.

Then there is the whole question of patriotism. When do we feel patriotic? It is obviously not an everyday emotion. But we are sedulously encouraged to be patriotic through school-books, through newspapers and other channels of propaganda, which stimulate racial egotism by praising national heroes and telling us that our own country and way of life are better than others. This patriotic spirit feeds our vanity from childhood to old age.

The constantly repeated assertion that we belong to a certain political or religious group, that we are of this nation or of that, flatters our little egos, puffs them out like sails, until we are ready to kill or be killed for our country, race or ideology. It is all so stupid and unnatural. Surely, human beings are more important than national and ideological boundaries.

The separative spirit of nationalism is spreading like fire

all over the world. Patriotism is cultivated and cleverly exploited by those who are seeking further expansion, wider powers, greater enrichment; and each one of us takes part in this process, for we also desire these things. Conquering other lands and other people provides new markets for goods as well as for political and religious ideologies.

One must look at all these expressions of violence and antagonism with an unprejudiced mind, that is, with a mind that does not identify itself with any country, race or ideology, but tries to find out what is true. There is great joy in seeing a thing clearly without being influenced by the notions and instructions of others, whether they be the government, the specialists or the very learned. Once we really see that patriotism is a hindrance to human happiness, we do not have to struggle against this false emotion in ourselves, it has gone from us forever.

Nationalism, the patriotic spirit, class and race consciousness, are all ways of the self, and therefore separative. After all, what is a nation but a group of individuals living together for economic and self-protective reasons? Out of fear and acquisitive self-defence arises the idea of "my country," with its boundaries and tariff walls, rendering brotherhood and the unity of man impossible.

The desire to gain and to hold, the longing to be identified with something greater than ourselves, creates the spirit of nationalism; and nationalism breeds war. In every country the government, encouraged by organized religion, is upholding nationalism and the separative spirit. Nationalism is a disease, and it can never bring about world unity. We cannot attain health through disease, we must first free ourselves from the disease.

It is because we are nationalists, ready to defend our sovereign States, our beliefs and acquisitions, that we must be perpetually armed. Property and ideas have become more important to us than human life, so there is constant antagonism and violence between ourselves and others. By maintaining the sovereignty of our country, we are destroying our sons; by worshipping the State, which is but a projection of ourselves, we are sacrificing our children to our own gratification. Nationalism and sovereign governments are the causes and the instruments of war.

Our present social institutions cannot evolve into a world federation, for their very foundations are unsound. Parliaments and systems of education which uphold national sovereignty and emphasize the importance of the group will never bring war to an end. Every separate group of people, with its rulers and its ruled, is a source of war. As long as we do not fundamentally alter the present relationship between man and man, industry will inevitably lead to confusion and become an instrument of destruction and misery; as long as there is violence and tyranny, deceit and propaganda, the brotherhood of man cannot be realized.

Merely to educate people to be wonderful engineers, brilliant scientists, capable executives, able workmen, will never bring the oppressors and the oppressed together; and we can see that our present system of education, which sustains the many causes that breed enmity and hatred between human beings, has not prevented mass murder in the name of one's country or in the name of God.

Organized religions, with their temporal and spiritual authority, are equally incapable of bringing peace to man, for they also are the outcome of our ignorance and fear, of our make-believe and egotism.

Craving security here or in the hereafter, we create institutions and ideologies which guarantee that security; but the more we struggle for security, the less we shall have it. The desire to be secure only fosters division and increases antagonism. If we deeply feel and understand the truth of this, not merely verbally or intellectually, but with our whole being, then we shall begin to alter fundamentally our relationship with our fellow-men in the immediate world about us; and only then is there a possibility of achieving unity and brotherhood.

Most of us are consumed by all sorts of fears, and are greatly concerned about our own security. We hope that, by some miracle, wars will come to an end, all the while accusing other national groups of being the instigators of war, as they in turn blame us for the disaster. Although war is so obviously detrimental to society, we prepare for war and develop in the young the military spirit.

But has military training any place in education? It all depends on what kind of human beings we want our children to be. If we want them to be efficient killers, then military training is necessary. If we want to discipline them and regiment their minds, if our purpose is to make them nationalistic and therefore irresponsible to society as a whole, then military training is a good way to do it. If we like death and destruction, military training is obviously important. It is the function of generals to plan and carry on war; and if our intention is to have constant battle between ourselves and our neighbours, then by all means let us have more generals.

If we are living only to have endless strife within ourselves and with others, if our desire is to perpetuate bloodshed and misery, then there must be more soldiers, more politicians, more enmity—which is what is actually happening. Modern civilization is based on violence, and is therefore courting death. As long as we worship force, violence will be our way of life. But if we want peace, if we want right relationship among men, whether Christian or Hindu, Russian or American, if we want our children to be integrated human beings, then military training is an absolute hindrance, it is the wrong way to set about it.

One of the chief causes of hatred and strife is the belief that a particular class or race is superior to another. The child is neither class nor race conscious; it is the home or school environment, or both, which makes him feel separative. In himself he does not care whether his playmate is a Negro or a Jew, a Brahmin or a non-Brahmin; but the influence of the whole social structure is continually impinging on his mind, affecting and shaping it.

Here again the problem is not with the child but with the adults, who have created a senseless environment of separatism and false values.

What real basis is there for differentiating between

human beings? Our bodies may be different in structure and color, our faces may be dissimilar, but inside the skin we are very much alike: proud, ambitious, envious, violent, sexual, power-seeking and so on. Remove the label and we are very naked; but we do not want to face our nakedness, and so we insist on the label—which indicates how immature, how really infantile we are.

To enable the child to grow up free from prejudice, one has first to break down all prejudice within oneself, and then in one's environment—which means breaking down the structure of this thoughtless society which we have created. At home we may tell the child how absurd it is to be conscious of one's class or race, and he will probably agree with us; but when he goes to school and plays with other children, he becomes contaminated by the separative spirit. Or it may be the other way around: the home may be traditional, narrow, and the school's influence may be broader. In either case there is a constant battle between the home and the school environments, and the child is caught between the two.

To raise a child sanely, to help him to be perceptive so that he sees through these stupid prejudices, we have to be in close relationship with him. We have to talk things over and let him listen to intelligent conversation; we have to encourage the spirit of inquiry and discontent which is already in him, thereby helping him to discover for himself what is true and what is false.

It is constant inquiry, true dissatisfaction, that brings creative intelligence; but to keep inquiry and discontent awake is extremely arduous, and most people do not want their children to have this kind of intelligence, for it is very uncomfortable to live with someone who is constantly questioning accepted values.

All of us are discontented when we are young, but unfortunately our discontent soon fades away, smothered by our imitative tendencies and our worship of authority. As we grow older, we begin to crystallize, to be satisfied and apprehensive. We become executives, priests, bank clerks, factory managers, technicians, and slow decay sets in. Because we desire to maintain our positions, we support the destructive society which has placed us there and given us some measure of security.

Government control of education is a calamity. There is no hope of peace and order in the world as long as education is the handmaid of the State or of organized religion. Yet more and more governments are taking charge of the children and their future; and if it is not the government, then it is the religious organizations which seek to control education.

This conditioning of the child's mind to fit a particular ideology, whether political or religious, breeds enmity between man and man. In a competitive society we cannot have brotherhood, and no reform, no dictatorship, no educational method can bring it about.

As long as you remain a New Zealander and I a Hindu, it is absurd to talk about the unity of man. How can we get together as human beings if you in your country, and I in mine, retain our respective religious prejudices and economic ways? How can there be brotherhood as long as patriotism is separating man from man, and millions are restricted by depressed economic conditions while others are well off? How can there be human unity when beliefs divide us, when there is domination of one group by another, when the rich are powerful and the poor are seeking that same power, when there is maldistribution of land, when some are well fed and multitudes are starving?

One of our difficulties is that we are not really in earnest about these matters, because we do not want to be greatly disturbed. We prefer to alter things only in a manner advantageous to ourselves, and so we are not deeply concerned about our own emptiness and cruelty.

Can we ever attain peace through violence? Is peace to be achieved gradually, through a slow process of time? Surely, love is not a matter of training or of time. The last two wars were fought for democracy, I believe; and now we are preparing for a still greater and more destructive war, and people are less free. But what would happen if we were to put aside such obvious hindrances to understanding as authority, belief, nationalism and the whole hierarchical spirit? We would be people without authority, human beings in direct relationship with one another—and then, perhaps, there would be love and compassion.

What is essential in education, as in every other field, is to have people who are understanding and affectionate, whose hearts are not filled with empty phrases, with the things of the mind.

If life is meant to be lived happily, with thought, with

care, with affection, then it is very important to understand ourselves; and if we wish to build a truly enlightened society, we must have educators who understand the ways of integration and who are therefore capable of imparting that understanding to the child.

Such educators would be a danger to the present structure of society. But we do not really want to build an enlightened society; and any teacher who, perceiving the full implications of peace, began to point out the true significance of nationalism and the stupidity of war, would soon lose his position. Knowing this, most teachers compromise, and thereby help to maintain the present system of exploitation and violence.

Surely, to discover truth, there must be freedom from strife, both within ourselves and with our neighbours. When we are not in conflict within ourselves, we are not in conflict outwardly. It is the inward strife which, projected outwardly, becomes the world conflict.

War is the spectacular and bloody projection of our everyday living. We precipitate war out of our daily lives; and without a transformation in ourselves, there are bound to be national and racial antagonisms, the childish quarrelling over ideologies, the multiplication of soldiers, the saluting of flags, and all the many brutalities that go to create organized murder.

Education throughout the world has failed, it has produced mounting destruction and misery. Governments are training the young to be the efficient soldiers and technicians they need; regimentation and prejudice are being cultivated and enforced. Taking these facts into consideration, we have to inquire into the meaning of existence and the significance and purpose of our lives. We have to discover the beneficent ways of creating a new environment; for environment can make the child a brute, an unfeeling specialist, or help him to become a sensitive, intelligent human being. We have to create a world government which is radically different, which is not based on nationalism, on ideologies, on force.

All this implies the understanding of our responsibility to one another in relationship; but to understand our responsibility, there must be love in our hearts, not mere learning or knowledge. The greater our love, the deeper will be its influence on society. But we are all brains and no heart; we cultivate the intellect and despise humility. If we really loved our children, we would want to save and protect them, we would not let them be sacrificed in wars.

I think we really want arms; we like the show of military power, the uniforms, the rituals, the drinks, the noise, the violence. Our everyday life is a reflection in miniature of this same brutal superficiality, and we are destroying one another through envy and thoughtlessness.

We want to be rich; and the richer we get, the more ruthless we become, even though we may contribute large sums to charity and education. Having robbed the victim, we return to him a little of the spoils, and this we call philanthropy. I do not think we realize what catastrophes we are preparing. Most of us live each day as rapidly and thoughtlessly as possible, and leave to the governments, to the cunning politicians, the direction of our lives.

All sovereign governments must prepare for war, and one's own government is no exception. To make its citizens efficient for war, to prepare them to perform their duties effectively, the government must obviously control and dominate them. They must be educated to act as machines, to be ruthlessly efficient. If the purpose and end of life is to destroy or be destroyed, then education *must* encourage ruthlessness; and I am not at all sure that that is not what we inwardly desire, for ruthlessness goes with the worship of success.

The sovereign State does not want its citizens to be free, to think for themselves, and it controls them through propaganda, through distorted historical interpretations and so on. That is why education is becoming more and more a means of teaching *what* to think and not *how* to think. If we were to think independently of the prevailing political system, we would be dangerous; free institutions might turn out pacifists or people who think contrary to the existing regime.

Right education is obviously a danger to sovereign governments—and so it is prevented by crude or subtle means. Education and food in the hands of the few have become the means of controlling man; and governments, whether of the left or of the right, are unconcerned as long as we are efficient machines for turning out merchandise and bullets.

Now, the fact that this is happening the world over means that we who are the citizens and educators, and who are responsible for the existing governments, do *not* fundamentally care whether there is freedom or slavery, peace or war, well-being or misery for man. We want a little reform here and there, but most of us are afraid to tear down the present society and build a completely new structure, for this would require a radical transformation of ourselves.

On the other hand, there are those who seek to bring about a violent revolution. Having helped to build the existing social order with all its conflicts, confusion and misery, they now desire to organize a perfect society. But can any of us organize a perfect society when it is we who have brought into being the present one? To believe that peace can be achieved through violence is to sacrifice the present for a future ideal; and this seeking of a right end through wrong means is one of the causes of the present disaster.

The expansion and predominance of sensate values necessarily creates the poison of nationalism, of economic frontiers, sovereign governments and the patriotic spirit, all of which excludes man's co-operation with man and corrupts human relationship, which is society. Society is the relationship between you and another; and without deeply understanding this relationship, not at any one level, but integrally, as a total process, we are bound to create again the same kind of social structure, however superficially modified.

If we are to change radically our present human relationship, which has brought untold misery to the world, our only and immediate task is to transform ourselves through self-knowledge. So we come back to the central point, which is oneself; but we dodge that point and shift the responsibility onto governments, religions and ideologies. The government is what *we* are, religions and ideologies are but a projection of ourselves; and until *we* change fundamentally there can be neither right education nor a peaceful world.

Outward security for all can come only when there is love and intelligence; and since we have created a world of conflict and misery in which outward security is rapidly becoming impossible for anyone, does it not indicate the utter futility of past and present education? As parents and teachers it is our direct responsibility to break away from traditional thinking, and not merely rely on the experts and their findings. Efficiency in technique has given us a certain capacity to earn money, and that is why most of us are satisfied with the present social structure; but the true educator is concerned only with right living, right education, and right means of livelihood.

The more irresponsible we are in these matters, the more the State takes over all responsibility. We are confronted, not with a political or economic crisis, but with a crisis of human deterioration which no political party or economic system can avert.

Another and still greater disaster is approaching dangerously close, and most of us are doing nothing whatever about it. We go on day after day exactly as before; we do not want to strip away all our false values and begin anew. We want to do patchwork reform, which only leads to problems of still further reform. But the building is crumbling, the walls are giving way, and fire is destroying it. We must leave the building and start on new ground, with different foundations, different values.

We cannot discard technical knowledge, but we can become inwardly aware of our ugliness, of our ruthlessness, of our deceptions and dishonesty, our utter lack of love. Only by intelligently freeing ourselves from the spirit of nationalism, from envy and the thirst for power, can a new social order be established.

Peace is not to be achieved by patchwork reform, nor by a mere rearrangement of old ideas and superstitions. There can be peace only when we understand what lies beyond the superficial, and thereby stop this wave of destruction which has been unleashed by our own aggressiveness and fears; and only then will there be hope for our children and salvation for the world.

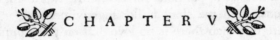

CHAPTER V

THE SCHOOL

THE right kind of education is concerned with individual freedom, which alone can bring true co-operation with the whole, with the many; but this freedom is not achieved through the pursuit of one's own aggrandizement and success. Freedom comes with self-knowledge, when the mind goes above and beyond the hindrances it has created for itself through craving its own security.

It is the function of education to help each individual to discover all these psychological hindrances, and not merely impose upon him new patterns of conduct, new modes of thought. Such impositions will never awaken intelligence, creative understanding, but will only further condition the individual. Surely, this is what is happening throughout the world, and that is why our problems continue and multiply.

It is only when we begin to understand the deep significance of human life that there can be true education; but to understand, the mind must intelligently free itself from the

83

self learning activities

desire for reward which breeds fear and conformity. If we regard our children as personal property, if to us they are the continuance of our petty selves and the fulfilment of our ambitions, then we shall build an environment, a social structure in which there is no love, but only the pursuit of self-centered advantages.

A school which is successful in the worldly sense is more often than not a failure as an educational center. A large and flourishing institution in which hundreds of children are educated together, with all its accompanying show and success, can turn out bank clerks and super-salesmen, industrialists or commissars, superficial people who are technically efficient; but there is hope only in the integrated individual, which only small schools can help to bring about. That is why it is far more important to have schools with a limited number of boys and girls and the right kind of educators, than to practise the latest and best methods in large institutions.

Unfortunately, one of our confusing difficulties is that we think we must operate on a huge scale. Most of us want large schools with imposing buildings, even though they are obviously not the right kind of educational centers, because we want to transform or affect what we call the masses.

But who are the masses? You and I. Let us not get lost in the thought that the masses must also be rightly educated. The consideration of the mass is a form of escape from immediate action. Right education will become universal if we begin with the immediate, if we are aware of ourselves in our relationship with our children, with our friends and neighbours. Our own action in the world we live in, in the world of our family and friends, will have expanding influence and effect.

By being fully aware of ourselves in all our relationships we shall begin to discover those confusions and limitations within us of which we are now ignorant; and in being aware of them, we shall understand and so dissolve them. Without this awareness and the self-knowledge which it brings, any reform in education or in other fields will only lead to further antagonism and misery.

[Being Aware]

In building enormous institutions and employing teachers who depend on a system instead of being alert and observant in their relationship with the individual student, we merely encourage the accumulation of facts, the development of capacity, and the habit of thinking mechanically, according to a pattern; but certainly none of this helps the student to grow into an integrated human being. Systems may have a limited use in the hands of alert and thoughtful educators, but they do not make for intelligence. Yet it is strange that words like "system," "institution," have become very important to us. Symbols have taken the place of reality, and we are content that it should be so; for reality is disturbing, while shadows give comfort.

Nothing of fundamental value can be accomplished through mass instruction, but only through the careful study and understanding of the difficulties, tendencies and capacities of each child; and those who are aware of this, and who earnestly desire to understand themselves and help the young, should come together and start a school that will

— Caring

have vital significance in the child's life by helping him to be integrated and intelligent. To start such a school, they need not wait until they have the necessary means. One can be a true teacher at home, and opportunities will come to the earnest.

Those who love their own children and the children about them, and who are therefore in earnest, will see to it that a right school is started somewhere around the corner, or in their own home. Then the money will come—it is the least important consideration. To maintain a small school of the right kind is of course financially difficult; it can flourish only on self-sacrifice, not on a fat bank account. Money invariably corrupts unless there is love and understanding. But if it is really a worth-while school, the necessary help will be found. When there is love of the child, all things are possible.

As long as the institution is the most important consideration, the child is not. The right kind of educator is concerned with the individual, and not with the number of pupils he has; and such an educator will discover that he can have a vital and significant school which some parents will support. But the teacher must have the flame of interest; if he is lukewarm, he will have an institution like any other.

If parents really love their children, they will employ legislation and other means to establish small schools staffed with the right kind of educators; and they will not be deterred by the fact that small schools are expensive and the right kind of educators difficult to find.

86

The School

They should realize, however, that there will inevitably
be opposition from vested interests, from governments and
organized religions, because such schools are bound to be
deeply revolutionary. True revolution is not the violent
sort; it comes about through cultivating the integration and
intelligence of human beings who, by their very life, will
gradually create radical changes in society.

But it is of the utmost importance that all the teachers in
a school of this kind should come together voluntarily, without being persuaded or chosen; for voluntary freedom from
worldliness is the only right foundation for a true educational center. If the teachers are to help one another and the
students to understand right values, there must be constant
and alert awareness in their daily relationship.

In the seclusion of a small school one is apt to forget
that there is an outside world, with its ever-increasing conflict, destruction and misery. That world is not separate from
us. On the contrary, it is part of us, for we have made it
what it is; and that is why, if there is to be a fundamental
alteration in the structure of society, right education is the
first step.

Only right education, and not ideologies, leaders and
economic revolutions, can provide a lasting solution for our
problems and miseries; and to see the truth of this fact is
not a matter of intellectual or emotional persuasion, nor of
cunning argument.

If the nucleus of the staff in a school of the right kind is
dedicated and vital, it will gather to itself others of the same
purpose, and those who are not interested will soon find

themselves out of place. If the center is purposive and alert, the indifferent periphery will wither and drop away; but if the center is indifferent, then the whole group will be uncertain and weak.

The center cannot be made up of the head-master alone. Enthusiasm or interest that depends on one person is sure to wane and die. Such interest is superficial, flighty and worthless, for it can be diverted and made subservient to the whims and fancies of another. If the head-master is dominating, then the spirit of freedom and co-operation obviously cannot exist. A strong character may build a first-rate school, but fear and subservience creep in, and then it generally happens that the rest of the staff is composed of non-entities.

Such a group is not conducive to individual freedom and understanding. The staff should not be under the domination of the head-master, and the head-master should not assume all the responsibility; on the contrary, each teacher should feel responsible for the whole. If there are only a few who are interested, then the indifference or opposition of the rest will impede or stultify the general effort.

One may doubt that a school can be run without a central authority; but one really does not know, because it has never been tried. Surely, in a group of true educators, this problem of authority will never arise. When all are endeavouring to be free and intelligent, co-operation with one another is possible at all levels. To those who have not given themselves over deeply and lastingly to the task of right education, the lack of a central authority may appear to be an impractical theory; but if one is completely dedicated to right education, then one does not require to be urged, directed or controlled. Intelligent teachers are pliable in the exercise of their capacities; attempting to be individually free, they abide by the regulations and do what is necessary for the benefit of the whole school. Serious interest is the beginning of capacity, and both are strengthened by application.

If one does not understand the psychological implications of obedience, merely to decide not to follow authority will only lead to confusion. Such confusion is not due to the absence of authority, but to the lack of deep and mutual interest in right education. If there is real interest, there is constant and thoughtful adjustment on the part of every teacher to the demands and necessities of running a school. In any relationship, frictions and misunderstandings are inevitable; but they become exaggerated when there is not the binding affection of common interest.

There must be unstinted co-operation among all the teachers in a school of the right kind. The whole staff should meet often, to talk over the various problems of the school; and when they have agreed upon a certain course of action, there should obviously be no difficulty in carrying out what has been decided. If some decision taken by the majority does not meet with the approval of a particular teacher, it can be discussed again at the next meeting of the faculty.

— growth

No teacher should be afraid of the head-master, nor should the head-master feel intimidated by the older teachers. Happy agreement is possible only when there is a feeling of absolute equality among all. It is essential that this feeling of equality prevail in the right kind of school, for there can be real co-operation only when the sense of superiority and its opposite are non-existent. If there is mutual trust, any difficulty or misunderstanding will not just be brushed aside, but will be faced, and confidence restored.

If the teachers are not sure of their own vocation and interest, there is bound to be envy and antagonism among them, and they will expend whatever energies they have over trifling details and wasteful bickerings; whereas, irritations and superficial disagreements will quickly be passed over if there is a burning interest in bringing about the right kind of education. Then the details which loom so large assume their normal proportions, friction and personal antagonisms are seen to be vain and destructive, and all talks and discussions help one to find out *what* is right and not *who* is right.

Difficulties and misunderstandings should always be talked over by those who are working together with a common intention, for it helps to clarify any confusion that may exist in one's own thinking. When there is purposive interest, there is also frankness and comradeship among the teachers, and antagonism can never arise between them; but if that interest is lacking, though superficially they may co-operate for their mutual advantage, there will always be conflict and enmity.

There may be, of course, other factors that are causing friction among the members of the staff. One teacher may be overworked, another may have personal or family worries, and perhaps still others do not feel deeply interested in

90

what they are doing. Surely, all these problems can be thrashed out at the teachers' meeting, for mutual interest makes for co-operation. It is obvious that nothing vital can be created if a few do everything and the rest sit back.

Equal distribution of work gives leisure to all, and each one must obviously have a certain amount of leisure. An overworked teacher becomes a problem to himself and to others. If one is under too great a strain, one is apt to become lethargic, indolent, and especially so if one is doing something which is not to one's liking. Recuperation is not possible if there is constant activity, physical or mental; but this question of leisure can be settled in a friendly manner acceptable to all.

What constitutes leisure differs with each individual. To some who are greatly interested in their work, that work itself is leisure; the very action of interest, such as study, is a form of relaxation. To others, leisure may be a withdrawal into seclusion.

If the educator is to have a certain amount of time to himself, he must be responsible only for the number of students that he can easily cope with. A direct and vital relationship between teacher and student is almost impossible when the teacher is weighed down by large and unmanageable numbers.

This is still another reason why schools should be kept small. It is obviously important to have a very limited number of students in a class, so that the educator can give his full attention to each one. When the group is too large he growth?

mass

cannot do this, and then punishment and reward become a convenient way of enforcing discipline.

The right kind of education is not possible *en masse*. To study each child requires patience, alertness and intelligence. To observe the child's tendencies, his aptitudes, his temperament, to understand his difficulties, to take into account his heredity and parental influence and not merely regard him as belonging to a certain category—all this calls for a swift and pliable mind, untrammelled by any system or prejudice. It calls for skill, intense interest and, above all, a sense of affection; and to produce educators endowed with these qualities is one of our major problems to-day.

The spirit of individual freedom and intelligence should pervade the whole school at all times. This can hardly be left to chance, and the casual mention at odd moments of the words "freedom" and "intelligence" has very little significance.

It is particularly important that students and teachers meet regularly to discuss all matters relating to the well-being of the whole group. A student council should be formed, on which the teachers are represented, which can thrash out all the problems of discipline, cleanliness, food and so on, and which can also help to guide any students who may be somewhat self-indulgent, indifferent or obstinate.

The students should choose from among themselves those who are to be responsible for the carrying out of decisions and for helping with the general supervision. After all, self-government in the school is a preparation for self-government in later life. If, while he is at school, the child learns to be considerate, impersonal and intelligent in any discussion pertaining to his daily problems, when he is older he will be able to meet effectively and dispassionately the greater and more complex trials of life. The school should encourage the children to understand one another's difficulties and peculiarities, moods and tempers; for then, as they grow up, they will be more thoughtful and patient in their relationship with others.

This same spirit of freedom and intelligence should be evident also in the child's studies. If he is to be creative and not merely an automaton, the student should not be encouraged to accept formulas and conclusions. Even in the study of a science, one should reason with him, helping him to see the problem in its entirety and to use his own judgment.

But what about guidance? Should there be no guidance whatsoever? The answer to this question depends on what is meant by "guidance." If in their hearts the teachers have put away all fear and all desire for domination, then they can help the student towards creative understanding and freedom; but if there is a conscious or unconscious desire to guide him towards a particular goal, then obviously they are hindering his development. Guidance towards a particular objective, whether created by oneself or imposed by another, impairs creativeness.

If the educator is concerned with the freedom of the individual, and not with his own preconceptions, he will help the child to discover that freedom by encouraging him to understand his own environment, his own temperament, his religious and family background, with all the influences and effects they can possibly have on him. If there is love and freedom in the hearts of the teachers themselves, they will approach each student mindful of his needs and difficulties; and then they will not be mere automatons, operating according to methods and formulas, but spontaneous human beings, ever alert and watchful.

Interest

The right kind of education should also help the student to discover what he is most interested in. If he does not find his true vocation, all his life will seem wasted; he will feel frustrated doing something which he does not want to do. If he wants to be an artist and instead becomes a clerk in some office, he will spend his life grumbling and pining away. So it is important for each one to find out what he wants to do, and then to see if it is worth doing. A boy may want to be a soldier; but before he takes up soldiering, he should be helped to discover whether the military vocation is beneficial to the whole of mankind.

Right education should help the student, not only to develop his capacities, but to understand his own highest interest. In a world torn by wars, destruction and misery, one must be able to build a new social order and bring about a different way of living.

The responsibility for building a peaceful and enlightened society rests chiefly with the educator, and it is obvious, without becoming emotionally stirred up about it, that he has a very great opportunity to help in achieving that social transformation. The right kind of education does not depend on the regulations of any government or the methods of any particular system; it lies in our own hands, in the hands of the parents and the teachers.

If parents really cared for their children, they would build a new society; but fundamentally most parents do not care, and so they have no time for this most urgent problem. They have time for making money, for amusements, for rituals and worship, but no time to consider what is the right kind of education for their children. This is a fact that the majority of people do not want to face. To face it might mean that they would have to give up their amusements and distractions, and certainly they are not willing to do that. So they send their children off to schools where the teacher cares no more for them than they do. Why should he care? Teaching is merely a job to him, a way of earning money.

The world we have created is so superficial, so artificial, so ugly if one looks behind the curtain; and we decorate the curtain, hoping that everything will somehow come right. Most people are unfortunately not very earnest about life except, perhaps, when it comes to making money, gaining power, or pursuing sexual excitement. They do not want to face the other complexities of life, and that is why, when their children grow up, they are as immature and unintegrated as their parents, constantly battling with themselves and with the world.

We say so easily that we love our children; but is there love in our hearts when we accept the existing social conditions, when we do not want to bring about a fundamental transformation in this destructive society? And as long as we

95

look to the specialists to educate our children, this confusion and misery will continue; for the specialists, being concerned with the part and not with the whole, are themselves unintegrated.

Instead of being the most honoured and responsible occupation, education is now considered slightingly, and most educators are fixed in a routine. They are not really concerned with integration and intelligence, but with the imparting of information; and a man who merely imparts information with the world crashing about him is not an educator.

An educator is not merely a giver of information; he is one who points the way to wisdom, to truth. Truth is far more important than the teacher. The search for truth is religion, and truth is of no country, of no creed, it is not to be found in any temple, church or mosque. Without the search for truth, society soon decays. To create a new society, each one of us has to be a true teacher, which means that we have to be both the pupil and the master; we have to educate ourselves.

If a new social order is to be established, those who teach merely to earn a salary can obviously have no place as teachers. To regard education as a means of livelihood is to exploit the children for one's own advantage. In an enlightened society, teachers will have no concern for their own welfare, and the community will provide for their needs.

The true teacher is not he who has built up an impressive educational organization, nor he who is an instrument of the politicians, nor he who is bound to an ideal, a belief or a country. The true teacher is inwardly rich and therefore asks nothing for himself; he is not ambitious and seeks no power in any form; he does not use teaching as a means of acquiring position or authority, and therefore he is free from the compulsion of society and the control of governments. Such teachers have the primary place in an enlightened civilization, for true culture is founded, not on the engineers and technicians, but on the educators.

CHAPTER VI

PARENTS AND TEACHERS

THE right kind of education begins with the educator, who must understand himself and be free from established patterns of thought; for what he is, that he imparts. If he has not been rightly educated, what can he teach except the same mechanical knowledge on which he himself has been brought up? The problem, therefore, is not the child, but the parent and the teacher; the problem is to educate the educator.

If we who are the educators do not understand ourselves, if we do not understand our relationship with the child but merely stuff him with information and make him pass examinations, how can we possibly bring about a new kind of education? The pupil is there to be guided and helped; but if the guide, the helper is himself confused and narrow, nationalistic and theory-ridden, then naturally his pupil will be what he is, and education becomes a source of further confusion and strife.

If we see the truth of this, we will realize how important it is that we begin to educate ourselves rightly. To be concerned with our own re-education is far more necessary than to worry about the future well-being and security of the child.

To educate the educator—that is, to have him understand himself—is one of the most difficult undertakings, because most of us are already crystallized within a system of thought or a pattern of action; we have already given ourselves over to some ideology, to a religion, or to a particular standard of conduct. That is why we teach the child *what* to think and not *how* to think.

Moreover, parents and teachers are largely occupied with their own conflicts and sorrows. Rich or poor, most parents are absorbed in their personal worries and trials. They are not gravely concerned about the present social and moral deterioration, but only desire that their children shall be equipped to get on in the world. They are anxious about the future of their children, eager to have them educated to hold secure positions, or to marry well.

Contrary to what is generally believed, most parents do not love their children, though they talk of loving them. If parents really loved their children, there would be no emphasis laid on the family and the nation as opposed to the whole, which creates social and racial divisions between men and brings about war and starvation. It is really extraordinary that, while people are rigorously trained to be lawyers or doctors, they may become parents without undergoing any training whatsoever to fit them for this all-important task.

More often than not, the family, with its separate tendencies, encourages the general process of isolation, thereby becoming a deteriorating factor in society. It is only when there is love and understanding that the walls of isolation are broken down, and then the family is no longer a closed circle, it is neither a prison nor a refuge; then the parents are in communion, not only with their children, but also with their neighbours.

Being absorbed in their own problems, many parents shift to the teacher the responsibility for the well-being of their children; and then it is important that the educator help in the education of the parents as well.

He must talk to them, explaining that the confused state of the world mirrors their own individual confusion. He must point out that scientific progress in itself cannot bring about a radical change in existing values; that technical training, which is now called education, has not given man freedom or made him any happier; and that to condition the student to accept the present environment is not conducive to intelligence. He must tell them what he is attempting to do for their child, and how he is setting about it. He has to awaken the parents' confidence, not by assuming the authority of a specialist dealing with ignorant laymen, but by talking over with them the child's temperament, difficulties, aptitudes and so on.

If the teacher takes a real interest in the child as an individual, the parents will have confidence in him. In this process, the teacher is educating the parents as well as himself, while learning from them in return. Right education is a mutual task demanding patience, consideration and affection. Enlightened teachers in an enlightened community could work out this problem of how to bring up children, and experiments along these lines should be made on a small scale by interested teachers and thoughtful parents.

Do parents ever ask themselves why they have children? Do they have children to perpetuate their name, to carry on their property? Do they want children merely for the sake of their own delight, to satisfy their own emotional needs? If so, then the children become a mere projection of the desires and fears of their parents.

Can parents claim to love their children when, by educating them wrongly, they foster envy, enmity and ambition? Is it love that stimulates the national and racial antagonisms which lead to war, destruction and utter misery, that sets man against man in the name of religions and ideologies?

Many parents encourage the child in the ways of conflict and sorrow, not only by allowing him to be submitted to the wrong kind of education, but by the manner in which they conduct their own lives; and then, when the child grows up and suffers, they pray for him or find excuses for his behaviour. The suffering of parents for their children is a form of possessive self-pity which exists only when there is no love.

If parents love their children, they will not be nationalistic, they will not identify themselves with any country; for the worship of the State brings on war, which kills or maims their sons. If parents love their children, they will discover what is right relationship to property; for the possessive instinct has given property an enormous and false significance which is destroying the world. If parents love their children, they will not belong to any organized religion; for dogma and belief divide people into conflicting groups, creating antagonism between man and man. If parents love their children, they will do away with envy and strife, and will set about altering fundamentally the structure of present-day society.

As long as we want our children to be powerful, to have bigger and better positions, to become more and more successful, there is no love in our hearts; for the worship of success encourages conflict and misery. To love one's children is to be in complete communion with them; it is to see that they have the kind of education that will help them to be sensitive, intelligent and integrated.

The first thing a teacher must ask himself, when he decides that he wants to teach, is what exactly he means by teaching. Is he going to teach the usual subjects in the habitual way? Does he want to condition the child to become a cog in the social machine, or help him to be an integrated, creative human being, a threat to false values? And if the educator is to help the student to examine and understand the values and influences that surround him and of which he is a part, must he not be aware of them himself? If one is blind, can one help others to cross to the other shore?

Surely, the teacher himself must first begin to see. He must be constantly alert, intensely aware of his own thoughts and feelings, aware of the ways in which he is conditioned, aware of his activities and his responses; for out of this watchfulness comes intelligence, and with it a radical transformation in his relationship to people and to things.

Intelligence has nothing to do with the passing of examinations. Intelligence is the spontaneous perception which makes a man strong and free. To awaken intelligence in a child, we must begin to understand for ourselves what intelligence is; for how can we ask a child to be intelligent if we ourselves remain unintelligent in so many ways? The problem is not only the student's difficulties, but also our own: the cumulative fears, unhappiness and frustrations of which we are not free. In order to help the child to be intelligent, we have to break down within ourselves those hindrances which make us dull and thoughtless.

How can we teach children not to seek personal security if we ourselves are pursuing it? What hope is there for the child if we who are parents and teachers are not entirely vulnerable to life, if we erect protective walls around ourselves? To discover the true significance of this struggle for security, which is causing such chaos in the world, we must begin to awaken our own intelligence by being aware of our psychological processes; we must begin to question all the values which now enclose us.

We should not continue to fit thoughtlessly into the pattern in which we happen to have been brought up. How can there ever be harmony in the individual and so in society if we do not understand ourselves? Unless the educator understands himself, unless he sees his own condi-

tioned responses and is beginning to free himself from
existing values, how can he possibly awaken intelligence in
the child? And if he cannot awaken intelligence in the
child, then what is his function?

It is only by understanding the ways of our own thought
and feeling that we can truly help the child to be a free
human being; and if the educator is vitally concerned with
this, he will be keenly aware, not only of the child, but also
of himself.

Very few of us observe our own thoughts and feelings.
If they are obviously ugly, we do not understand their full
significance, but merely try to check them or push them
aside. We are not deeply aware of ourselves; our thoughts
and feelings are stereotyped, automatic. We learn a few
subjects, gather some information, and then try to pass it on
to the children.

But if we are vitally interested, we shall not only try to
find out what experiments are being made in education
in different parts of the world, but we shall want to be very
clear about our own approach to this whole question; we
shall ask ourselves why and to what purpose we are educating the children and ourselves; we shall inquire into the
meaning of existence, into the relationship of the individual
to society, and so on. Surely, educators must be aware of
these problems and try to help the child to discover the
truth concerning them, without projecting upon him their
own idiosyncrasies and habits of thought.

Merely to follow a system, whether political or educational, will never solve our many social problems; and it is

far more important to understand the manner of our approach to any problem, than to understand the problem itself.

If children are to be free from fear—whether of their parents, of their environment, or of God—the educator himself must have no fear. But that is the difficulty: to find teachers who are not themselves the prey of some kind of fear. Fear narrows down thought and limits initiative, and a teacher who is fearful obviously cannot convey the deep significance of being without fear. Like goodness, fear is contagious. If the educator himself is secretly afraid, he will pass that fear on to his students, although its contamination may not be immediately seen.

Suppose, for example, that a teacher is afraid of public opinion; he sees the absurdity of his fear, and yet cannot go beyond it. What is he to do? He can at least acknowledge it to himself, and can help his students to understand fear by bringing out his own psychological reaction and openly talking it over with them. This honest and sincere approach will greatly encourage the students to be equally open and direct with themselves and with the teacher.

To give freedom to the child, the educator himself must be aware of the implications and the full significance of freedom. Example and compulsion in any form do not help to bring about freedom, and it is only in freedom that there can be self-discovery and insight.

The child is influenced by the people and the things about him, and the right kind of educator should help him to uncover these influences and their true worth. Right values are not discovered through the authority of society or tradition; only individual thoughtfulness can reveal them.

If one understands this deeply, one will encourage the student from the very beginning to awaken insight into present-day individual and social values. One will encourage him to seek out, not any particular set of values, but the true value of all things. One will help him to be fearless, which is to be free of all domination, whether by the teacher, the family or society, so that as an individual he can flower in love and goodness. In thus helping the student towards freedom, the educator is changing his own values also; he too is beginning to be rid of the "me" and the "mine," he too is flowering in love and goodness. This process of mutual education creates an altogether different relationship between the teacher and the student.

Domination or compulsion of any kind is a direct hindrance to freedom and intelligence. The right kind of educator has no authority, no power in society; he is beyond the edicts and sanctions of society. If we are to help the student to be free from his hindrances, which have been created by himself and by his environment, then every form of compulsion and domination must be understood and put aside; and this cannot be done if the educator is not also freeing himself from all crippling authority.

To follow another, however great, prevents the discovery of the ways of the self; to run after the promise of some ready-made Utopia makes the mind utterly unaware of the enclosing action of its own desire for comfort, for authority, for someone else's help. The priest, the politician, the lawyer, the soldier, are all there to "help" us; but such help destroys intelligence and freedom. The help we need does not lie outside ourselves. We do not have to beg for help; it comes without our seeking it when we are humble in our dedicated work, when we are open to the understanding of our daily trials and accidents.

We must avoid the conscious or unconscious craving for support and encouragement, for such craving creates its own response, which is always gratifying. It is comforting to have someone to encourage us, to give us a lead, to pacify us; but this habit of turning to another as a guide, as an authority, soon becomes a poison in our system. The moment we depend on another for guidance, we forget our original intention, which was to awaken individual freedom and intelligence.

All authority is a hindrance, and it is essential that the educator should not become an authority for the student. The building up of authority is both a conscious and an unconscious process.

The student is uncertain, groping, but the teacher is sure in his knowledge, strong in his experience. The strength and certainty of the teacher give assurance to the student, who tends to bask in that sunlight; but such assurance is neither lasting nor true. A teacher who consciously or unconsciously encourages dependence can never be of great help to his students. He may overwhelm them with his knowledge, dazzle them with his personality, but he is not the right kind of educator because his knowledge and experiences are his addiction, his security, his prison; and until he himself is free of them, he cannot help his students to be integrated human beings.

To be the right kind of educator, a teacher must constantly be freeing himself from books and laboratories; he must ever be watchful to see that the students do not make of him an example, an ideal, an authority. When the teacher desires to fulfil himself in his students, when their success is his, then his teaching is a form of self-continuation, which is detrimental to self-knowledge and freedom. The right kind of educator must be aware of all these hindrances in order to help his students to be free, not only from his authority, but from their own self-enclosing pursuits.

Unfortunately, when it comes to understanding a problem, most teachers do not treat the student as an equal partner; from their superior position, they give instructions to the pupil, who is far below them. Such a relationship only strengthens fear in both the teacher and the student. What creates this unequal relationship? Is it that the teacher is afraid of being found out? Does he keep a dignified distance to guard his susceptibilities, his importance? Such superior aloofness in no way helps to break down the barriers that separate individuals. After all, the educator and his pupil are helping each other to educate themselves.

All relationship should be a mutual education; and as the protective isolation afforded by knowledge, by achievement, by ambition, only breeds envy and antagonism, the right kind of educator must transcend these walls with which he surrounds himself.

Because he is devoted solely to the freedom and integration of the individual, the right kind of educator is deeply and truly religious. He does not belong to any sect, to any organized religion; he is free of beliefs and rituals, for he knows that they are only illusions, fancies, superstitions projected by the desires of those who create them. He knows that reality or God comes into being only when there is self-knowledge and therefore freedom.

People who have no academic degrees often make the best teachers because they are willing to experiment; not being specialists, they are interested in learning, in understanding life. For the true teacher, teaching is not a technique, it is his way of life; like a great artist, he would rather starve than give up his creative work. Unless one has this burning desire to teach, one should not be a teacher. It is of the utmost importance that one discover for oneself whether one has this gift, and not merely drift into teaching because it is a means of livelihood.

As long as teaching is only a profession, a means of livelihood, and not a dedicated vocation, there is bound to be a wide gap between the world and ourselves: our home life and our work remain separate and distinct. As long as education is only a job like any other, conflict and enmity among individuals and among the various class levels of society are inevitable; there will be increasing competition, the ruthless pursuit of personal ambition, and the building up of the national and racial divisions which create antagonism and endless wars.

But if we have dedicated ourselves to be the right kind of educators, we do not create barriers between our home life and the life at school, for we are everywhere concerned with freedom and intelligence. We consider equally the children of the rich and of the poor, regarding each child as an individual with his particular temperament, heredity, ambitions, and so on. We are concerned, not with a class, not with the powerful or the weak, but with the freedom and integration of the individual.

Dedication to the right kind of education must be wholly voluntary. It should not be the result of any kind of persuasion, or of any hope of personal gain; and it must be devoid of the fears that arise from the craving for success and achievement. The identification of oneself with the success or failure of a school is still within the field of personal motive. If to teach is one's vocation, if one looks upon the right kind of education as a vital need for the individual, then one will not allow oneself to be hindered or in any way side-tracked either by one's own ambitions or by those of another; one will find time and opportunity for this work, and will set about it without seeking reward, honour or fame. Then all other things—family, personal security, comfort—become of secondary importance.

If we are in earnest about being the right kind of teachers, we shall be thoroughly dissatisfied, not with a particular system of education, but with all systems, because we see that no educational method can free the individual. A method or a system may condition him to a different set of values, but it cannot make him free.

One has to be very watchful also not to fall into one's own particular system, which the mind is ever building. To have a pattern of conduct, of action, is a convenient and safe procedure, and that is why the mind takes shelter within its formulations. To be constantly alert is bothersome and exacting, but to develop and follow a method does not demand thought.

Repetition and habit encourage the mind to be sluggish; a shock is needed to awaken it, which we then call a problem. We try to solve this problem according to our well-worn explanations, justifications and condemnations, all of which puts the mind back to sleep again. In this form of sluggishness the mind is constantly being caught, and the right kind of educator not only puts an end to it within himself, but also helps his students to be aware of it.

Some may ask, "How does one become the right kind of educator?" Surely, to ask "how" indicates, not a free mind, but a mind that is timorous, that is seeking an advantage, a result. The hope and the effort to become something only makes the mind conform to the desired end, while a free mind is constantly watching, learning, and therefore breaking through its self-projected hindrances.

Freedom is at the beginning, it is not something to be gained at the end. The moment one asks "how," one is confronted with insurmountable difficulties, and the teacher who is eager to dedicate his life to education will never ask this question, for he knows that there is no method by which one can become the right kind of educator. If one is vitally interested, one does not ask for a method that will assure one of the desired result.

Can any system make us intelligent? We may go through

the grind of a system, acquire degrees, and so on; but will we then be educators, or merely the personifications of a system? To seek reward, to want to be called an outstanding educator, is to crave recognition and praise; and while it is sometimes agreeable to be appreciated and encouraged, if one depends upon it for one's sustained interest, it becomes a drug of which one soon wearies. To expect appreciation and encouragement is quite immature.

If anything new is to be created, there must be alertness and energy, not bickerings and wrangles. If one feels frustrated in one's work, then boredom and weariness generally follow. If one is not interested, one should obviously not go on teaching.

But why is there so often a lack of vital interest among teachers? What causes one to feel frustrated? Frustration is not the result of being forced by circumstances to do this or that; it arises when we do not know for ourselves what it is that we really want to do. Being confused, we get pushed around, and finally land in something which has no appeal for us at all.

If teaching is our true vocation, we may feel temporarily frustrated because we have not seen a way out of this present educational confusion; but the moment we see and understand the implications of the right kind of education, we shall have again all the necessary drive and enthusiasm. It is not a matter of will or resolution, but of perception and understanding.

If teaching is one's vocation, and if one perceives the grave importance of the right kind of education, one cannot help but be the right kind of educator. There is no need to follow any method. The very fact of understanding that the right kind of education is indispensable if we are to achieve the freedom and integration of the individual, brings about a fundamental change in oneself. If one becomes aware that there can be peace and happiness for man only through right education, then one will naturally give one's whole life and interest to it.

One teaches because one wants the child to be rich inwardly, which will result in his giving right value to possessions. Without inner richness, worldly things become extravagantly important, leading to various forms of destruction and misery. One teaches to encourage the student to find his true vocation, and to avoid those occupations that foster antagonism between man and man. One teaches to help the young towards self-knowledge, without which there can be no peace, no lasting happiness. One's teaching is not self-fulfilment, but self-abnegation.

Without the right kind of teaching, illusion is taken for reality, and then the individual is ever in conflict within himself, and therefore there is conflict in his relationship with others, which is society. One teaches because one sees that self-knowledge alone, and not the dogmas and rituals of organized religion, can bring about a tranquil mind; and that creation, truth, God, comes into being only when the "me" and the "mine" are transcended.

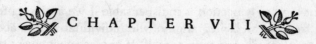

CHAPTER VII

SEX AND MARRIAGE

LIKE other human problems, the problem of our passions and sexual urges is a complex and difficult one, and if the educator himself has not deeply probed into it and seen its many implications, how can he help those he is educating? If the parent or the teacher is himself caught up in the turmoils of sex, how can he guide the child? Can we help the children if we ourselves do not understand the significance of this whole problem? The manner in which the educator imparts an understanding of sex depends on the state of his own mind; it depends on whether he is gently dispassionate, or consumed by his own desires.

Now, why is sex to most of us a problem, full of confusion and conflict? Why has it become a dominant factor in our lives? One of the main reasons is that we are not creative; and we are not creative because our whole social and moral culture, as well as our educational methods, are based on development of the intellect. The solution to this problem of sex lies in understanding that creation does not occur through the functioning of the intellect. On the contrary, there is creation only when the intellect is still.

The intellect, the mind as such, can only repeat, recollect, it is constantly spinning new words and rearranging old ones; and as most of us feel and experience only through the brain, we live exclusively on words and mechanical repetitions. This is obviously not creation; and since we are uncreative, the only means of creativeness left to us is sex. Sex is of the mind, and that which is of the mind must fulfil itself or there is frustration.

Our thoughts, our lives are bright, arid, hollow, empty; emotionally we are starved, religiously and intellectually we are repetitive, dull; socially, politically and economically we are regimented, controlled. We are not happy people, we are not vital, joyous; at home, in business, at church, at school, we never experience a creative state of being, there is no deep release in our daily thought and action. Caught and held from all sides, naturally sex becomes our only outlet, an experience to be sought again and again because it momentarily offers that state of happiness which comes when there is absence of self. It is not sex that constitutes a problem, but the desire to recapture the state of happiness, to gain and maintain pleasure, whether sexual or any other.

What we are really searching for is this intense passion of self-forgetfulness, this identification with something in which we can lose ourselves completely. Because the self is small, petty and a source of pain, consciously or unconsciously we want to lose ourselves in individual or collective.

excitement, in lofty thoughts, or in some gross form of sensation.

When we seek to escape from the self, the means of escape are very important, and then they also become painful problems to us. Unless we investigate and understand the hindrances that prevent creative living, which is freedom from self, we shall not understand the problem of sex.

One of the hindrances to creative living is fear, and respectability is a manifestation of that fear. The respectable, the morally bound, are not aware of the full and deep significance of life. They are enclosed between the walls of their own righteousness and cannot see beyond them. Their stained-glass morality, based on ideals and religious beliefs, has nothing to do with reality; and when they take shelter behind it, they are living in the world of their own illusions. In spite of their self-imposed and gratifying morality, the respectable also are in confusion, misery and conflict.

Fear, which is the result of our desire to be secure, makes us conform, imitate and submit to domination, and therefore it prevents creative living. To live creatively is to live in freedom, which is to be without fear; and there can be a state of creativeness only when the mind is not caught up in desire and the gratification of desire. It is only by watching our own hearts and minds with delicate attention that we can unravel the hidden ways of our desire. The more thoughtful and affectionate we are, the less desire dominates the mind. It is only when there is no love that sensation becomes a consuming problem.

To understand this problem of sensation, we shall have

to approach it, not from any one direction, but from every side, the educational, the religious, the social and the moral. Sensations have become almost exclusively important to us because we lay such overwhelming emphasis on sensate values.

Through books, through advertisements, through the cinema, and in many other ways, various aspects of sensation are constantly being stressed. The political and religious pageants, the theatre and other forms of amusement, all encourage us to seek stimulation at different levels of our being; and we delight in this encouragement. Sensuality is being developed in every possible way, and at the same time, the ideal of chastity is upheld. A contradiction is thus built up within us; and strangely enough, this very contradiction is stimulating.

It is only when we understand the pursuit of sensation, which is one of the major activities of the mind, that pleasure, excitement and violence cease to be a dominant feature in our lives. It is because we do not love, that sex, the pursuit of sensation, has become a consuming problem. When there is love, there is chastity; but he who *tries* to be chaste, is not. Virtue comes with freedom, it comes when there is an understanding of what *is*.

When we are young, we have strong sexual urges, and most of us try to deal with these desires by controlling and disciplining them, because we think that without some kind of restraint we shall become consumingly lustful. Organized religions are much concerned about our sexual morality; but they allow us to perpetrate violence and murder in the

117

name of patriotism, to indulge in envy and crafty ruthlessness, and to pursue power and success. Why should they
be so concerned with this particular type of morality, and
not attack exploitation, greed and war? Is it not because
organized religions, being part of the environment which we
have created, depend for their very existence on our fears
and hopes, on our envy and separatism? So, in the religious
field as in every other, the mind is held in the projections
of its own desires.

As long as there is no deep understanding of the whole
process of desire, the institution of marriage as it now exists,
whether in the East or in the West, cannot provide the
answer to the sexual problem. Love is not induced by the
signing of a contract, nor is it based on an exchange of
gratification, nor on mutual security and comfort. All these
things are of the mind, and that is why love occupies so
small a place in our lives. Love is not of the mind, it is
wholly independent of thought with its cunning calcula-
tions, its self-protective demands and reactions. When there
is love, sex is never a problem—it is the lack of love that
creates the problem.

The hindrances and escapes of the mind constitute the
problem, and not sex or any other specific issue; and that is
why it is important to understand the mind's process, its
attractions and repulsions, its responses to beauty, to ugliness. We should observe ourselves, become aware of how
we regard people, how we look at men and women. We
should see that the family becomes a center of separatism
and of anti-social activities when it is used as a means of

self-perpetuation, for the sake of one's self-importance. Family and property, when centered on the self with its ever-narrowing desires and pursuits, become the instruments of power and domination, a source of conflict between the individual and society.

The difficulty in all these human questions is that we ourselves, the parents and teachers, have become so utterly weary and hopeless, altogether confused and without peace; life weighs heavily upon us, and we want to be comforted, we want to be loved. Being poor and insufficient within ourselves, how can we hope to give the right kind of education to the child?

That is why the major problem is not the pupil, but the educator; our own hearts and minds must be cleansed if we are to be capable of educating others. If the educator himself is confused, crooked, lost in a maze of his own desires, how can he impart wisdom or help to make straight the way of another? But we are not machines to be understood and repaired by experts; we are the result of a long series of influences and accidents, and each one has to unravel and understand for himself the confusion of his own nature.

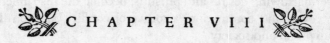

CHAPTER VIII

ART, BEAUTY AND CREATION

MOST of us are constantly trying to escape from ourselves; and as art offers a respectable and easy means of doing so, it plays a significant part in the lives of many people. In the desire for self-forgetfulness, some turn to art, others take to drink, while still others follow mysterious and fanciful religious doctrines.

When, consciously or unconsciously, we use something to escape from ourselves, we become addicted to it. To depend on a person, a poem, or what you will, as a means of release from our worries and anxieties, though momentarily enriching, only creates further conflict and contradiction in our lives.

The state of creativeness cannot exist where there is conflict, and the right kind of education should therefore help the individual to face his problems and not glorify the ways of escape; it should help him to understand and eliminate conflict, for only then can this state of creativeness come into being.

Art, Beauty and Creation

Art divorced from life has no great significance. When art is separate from our daily living, when there is a gap between our instinctual life and our efforts on canvas, in marble or in words, then art becomes merely an expression of our superficial desire to escape from the reality of what *is*. To bridge this gap is very arduous, especially for those who are gifted and technically proficient; but it is only when the gap is bridged that our life becomes integrated and art an integral expression of ourselves.

Mind has the power to create illusion; and without understanding its ways, to seek inspiration is to invite self-deception. Inspiration comes when we are open to it, not when we are courting it. To attempt to gain inspiration through any form of stimulation leads to all kinds of delusions.

Unless one is aware of the significance of existence, capacity or gift gives emphasis and importance to the self and its cravings. It tends to make the individual self-centered and separative; he feels himself to be an entity apart, a superior being, all of which breeds many evils and causes ceaseless strife and pain. The self is a bundle of many entities, each opposed to the others. It is a battlefield of conflicting desires, a center of constant struggle between the "mine" and the "not-mine"; and as long as we give importance to the self, to the "me" and the "mine," there will be increasing conflict within ourselves and in the world.

A true artist is beyond the vanity of the self and its ambitions. To have the power of brilliant expression, and yet be caught in worldly ways, makes for a life of contradiction and strife. Praise and adulation, when taken to heart, inflate the ego and destroy receptivity, and the worship of success in any field is obviously detrimental to intelligence.

Any tendency or talent which makes for isolation, any form of self-identification, however stimulating, distorts the expression of sensitivity and brings about insensitivity. Sensitivity is dulled when gift becomes personal, when importance is given to the "me" and the "mine"—*I* paint, *I* write, *I* invent. It is only when *we* are aware of every movement of our own thought and feeling in our relationship with people, with things and with nature, that the mind is open, pliable, not tethered to self-protective demands and pursuits; and only then is there sensitivity to the ugly and the beautiful, unhindered by the self.

Sensitivity to beauty and to ugliness does not come about through attachment; it comes with love, when there are no self-created conflicts. When we are inwardly poor, we indulge in every form of outward show, in wealth, power and possessions. When our hearts are empty, we collect things. If we can afford it, we surround ourselves with objects that we consider beautiful, and because we attach enormous importance to them, we are responsible for much misery and destruction.

The acquisitive spirit is not the love of beauty; it arises from the desire for security, and to be secure is to be insensitive. The desire to be secure creates fear; it sets going a process of isolation which builds walls of resistance around us, and these walls prevent all sensitivity. However beautiful an object may be, it soon loses its appeal for us; we get used to it, and that which was a joy becomes empty and dull. Beauty is still there, but we are no longer open to it, and it has been absorbed into our monotonous daily existence.

Since our hearts are withered and we have forgotten how to be kindly, how to look at the stars, at the trees, at the reflections on the water, we require the stimulation of pictures and jewels, of books and endless amusements. We are constantly seeking new excitements, new thrills, we crave an ever-increasing variety of sensations. It is this craving and its satisfaction that make the mind and heart weary and dull. As long as we are seeking sensation, the things that we call beautiful and ugly have but a very superficial significance. There is lasting joy only when we are capable of approaching all things afresh—which is not possible as long as we are bound up in our desires. The craving for sensation and gratification prevents the experiencing of that which is always new. Sensations can be bought, but not the love of beauty.

When we are aware of the emptiness of our own minds and hearts without running away from it into any kind of stimulation or sensation, when we are completely open, highly sensitive, only then can there be creation, only then shall we find creative joy. To cultivate the outer without understanding the inner must inevitably build up those values which lead men to destruction and sorrow.

Learning a technique may provide us with a job, but it will not make us creative; whereas, if there is joy, if there is the creative fire, it will find a way to express itself, one need not study a method of expression. When one really wants to write a poem, one writes it, and if one has the technique, so much the better; but why stress what is but a means of communication if one has nothing to say? When there is love in our hearts, we do not search for a way of putting words together.

Great artists and great writers may be creators, but we are not, we are mere spectators. We read vast numbers of books, listen to magnificent music, look at works of art, but we never directly experience the sublime; our experience is always through a poem, through a picture, through the personality of a saint. To sing we must have a song in our hearts; but having lost the song, we pursue the singer. Without an intermediary we feel lost; but we *must* be lost before we can discover anything. Discovery is the beginning of creativeness; and without creativeness, do what we may, there can be no peace or happiness for man.

We think that we shall be able to live happily, creatively, if we learn a method, a technique, a style; but creative happiness comes only when there is inward richness, it can never be attained through any system. Self-improvement, which is another way of assuring the security of the "me" and the "mine," is not creative, nor is it love of beauty. Creativeness comes into being when there is constant awareness of the ways of the mind, and of the hindrances it has built for itself.

The freedom to create comes with self-knowledge; but self-knowledge is not a gift. One can be creative without having any particular talent. Creativeness is a state of

124

being in which the conflicts and sorrows of the self are absent, a state in which the mind is not caught up in the demands and pursuits of desire.

To be creative is not merely to produce poems, or statues, or children; it is to be in that state in which truth can come into being. Truth comes into being when there is a complete cessation of thought; and thought ceases only when the self is absent, when the mind has ceased to create, that is, when it is no longer caught in its own pursuits. When the mind is utterly still without being forced or trained into quiescence, when it is silent because the self is inactive, then there is creation.

The love of beauty may express itself in a song, in a smile, or in silence; but most of us have no inclination to be silent. We have not the time to observe the birds, the passing clouds, because we are too busy with our pursuits and pleasures. When there is no beauty in our hearts, how can we help the children to be alert and sensitive? We try to be sensitive to beauty while avoiding the ugly; but avoidance of the ugly makes for insensitivity. If we would develop sensitivity in the young, we ourselves must be sensitive to beauty and to ugliness, and must take every opportunity to awaken in them the joy there is in seeing, not only the beauty that man has created, but also the beauty of nature.